Im...
Tea...

Professional Learning

Series Editors: Ivor Goodson and Andy Hargreaves

The work of teachers has changed significantly in recent years and now, more than ever, there is a pressing need for high-quality professional development. This timely new series examines the actual and possible forms of professional learning, professional knowledge, professional development and professional standards that are beginning to emerge and be debated at the beginning of the twenty-first century. The series will be important reading for teachers, teacher educators, staff developers and policy makers throughout the English-speaking world.

Published and forthcoming titles:

Elizabeth Campbell: *The Ethical Teacher*
Martin Coles and Geoff Southworth: *Developing Leadership*
Ivor Goodson: *Professional Knowledge, Professional Lives*
Andy Hargreaves: *Teaching in the Knowledge Society*
Alma Harris and Daniel Muijs: *Improving Schools Through Teacher Leadership*
Garry Hoban: *Teacher Learning for Educational Change*
Bob Lingard, Debra Hayes, Martin Mills and Pam Christie: *Leading Learning*
Judyth Sachs: *The Activist Teaching Profession*

Improving Schools Through Teacher Leadership

Alma Harris and Daniel Muijs

Open University Press

Open University Press
McGraw-Hill Education
McGraw-Hill House
Shoppenhangers Road
Maidenhead
Berkshire
England
SL6 2QL

email: enquiries@openup.co.uk
world wide web: www.openup.co.uk

and Two Penn Plaza, New York, NY 10121-2289, USA

First published 2005

A catalogue record of this book is available from the British Library

ISBN 0335 20882 7 (pb) 0335 20883 5 (hb)

Library of Congress Cataloguing-in-Publication Data
CIP data applied for

Typeset by YHT Ltd, London
Printed in the UK by MPG Books, Bodmin, Cornwall

Contents

Series editors' preface

Teaching today is increasingly complex work, requiring the highest standards of professional practice to perform it well (Hargreaves and Goodson 1996). It is the core profession, the key agent of change in today's knowledge society. Teachers are the midwives of that knowledge society. Without them, or their competence, the future will be malformed and stillborn. In the United States, George W. Bush's educational slogan has been to leave no child behind. What is clear today in general, and in this book in particular, is that leaving no child behind means leaving no teacher or leader behind either. Yet, teaching too is also in crisis, staring tragedy in the face. There is a demographic exodus occurring in the profession as many teachers in the ageing cohort of the Boomer generation are retiring early because of stress, burnout or disillusionment with the impact of years of mandated reform on their lives and work. After a decade of relentless reform in a climate of shaming and blaming teachers for perpetuating poor standards, the attractiveness of teaching as a profession has faded fast among potential new recruits.

Teaching has to compete much harder against other professions for high calibre candidates than it did in the last period of mass recruitment – when able women were led to feel that only nursing and secretarial work were viable options. Teaching may not yet have reverted to being an occupation for 'unmarriageable women and unsaleable men' as Willard Waller described it in 1932, but many American inner cities now run their school systems on high numbers of uncertified teachers. The teacher recruitment crisis in England has led some schools to move to a four-day week; more and more schools are run on the increasingly casualized labour of temporary teachers from overseas, or endless supply teachers whose quality busy administrators do not always have time to monitor (Townsend 2001).

Meanwhile in the Canadian province of Ontario, in 2001, hard-nosed and hard-headed reform strategies led in a single year to a decrease in applications to teacher education programmes in faculties of education by 20-25 per cent, and a drop in a whole grade level of accepted applicants.

Amid all this despair and danger though, there remains great hope and some reasons for optimism about a future of learning that is tied in its vision to an empowering, imaginative and inclusive vision for teaching as well. The educational standards movement is showing visible signs of overreaching itself as people are starting to complain about teacher shortages in schools, and the loss of creativity and inspiration in classrooms (Hargreaves *et al.* 2001). There is growing international support for the resumption of more humane middle years philosophies in the early years of secondary school that put priority on community and engagement, alongside curriculum content and academic achievement. School districts in the United States are increasingly seeing that high quality professional development for teachers is absolutely indispensable to bringing about deep changes in student achievement (Fullan 2001). In England and Wales, policy documents and White Papers are similarly advocating for more 'earned autonomy', and schools and teachers are performing well (e.g. DfES 2001). Governments almost everywhere are beginning to speak more positively about teachers and teaching – bestowing honour and respect where blame and contempt had prevailed in the recent past.

The time has rarely been more opportune or more pressing to think more deeply about what professional learning, professional knowledge and professional status should look like for the new generation of teachers who will shape the next three decades of public education. Should professional learning accompany increased autonomy for teachers, or should its provision be linked to the evidence of demonstrated improvements in pupil achievement results? Do successful schools do better when the professional learning is self-guided, discretionary and intellectually challenging, while failing schools or schools in trouble benefit from required training in the skills that evidence shows can raise classroom achievement quickly? And does accommodating professional learning to the needs of different schools and their staffs constitute administrative sensitivity and flexibility (Hopkins *et al.* 1997), or a kind of professional development apartheid (Hargreaves, forthcoming)? These are the kinds of questions and issues which this series on professional learning sets out to address.

How effectively teachers pursue their own professional learning depends, of course, on their own interest and initiative. But the extent and effectiveness of professional learning is also influenced by the school communities in which teachers work. The leaders of these communities create the climate of encouragement and expectation in which teachers do or do not learn how to improve professionally. Helping teachers learn well so they can help pupils to learn well is one of the fundamental responsibilities of leadership – and one of the essential elements of professional learning among leaders themselves.

Alma Harris and Daniel Muij have both developed significant new perspectives on teacher leadership. Harris's recent work has shown how a key aspect of the conundrum of delivery of school improvement lies not in the widely advocated structural reforms but in cultural change: investment in professional learning and the generation of communities of practice and collaboration (Harris, 2002).

They argue that the balance of power in schooling discourse is moving from "Soulless Standardisation" and accountability towards more culturally nuanced ideas such as partnerships, networking and federations. At the moment these two discourses sit in uneasy and often contradictory tension. But as the balance shifts they note the 'old order' of leadership is likely to be increasingly replaced by a new order. Whether this shift in the 'orders' of leadership will be sustained without a significant shift in the world economic order remains a moot point. They argue

> "the 'old order' of leadership, equally headship is unlikely to prevail as the architecture of schooling becomes more diverse, complex and innovative. The 'new order' is premised upon a view of leadership that is distributed and empowers those closest to the classroom to undertake leadership tasks and actions" (p.11)

This validates their focus on teacher leadership which they explore in innovative and exciting ways.

The great virtue of *Improving Schools through Teacher Leadership* is its grounding a range of research projects undertaken by the authors notably the Gatsby Teacher Effectiveness Study (see Muij & Reynolds, 2000) and, most significantly, the study funded by the General Teaching Council (in association with the National Union of Teachers) on teacher leadership (see Harris & Muij, 2003).

The latter study is dealt with in substantial detail (in Chapter 9). Their summary is a model of precision and concision with sections on understanding teacher leadership recognising teacher leadership and on the benefits of such leadership. The section on enhancing teacher leadership with its cultural emphasis and focus on supportive cultures and communities of professional practice is a model of its kind and should provide important signposts for those developing teacher leadership.

What readers will find most appealing of all about the book we suspect is its tone of humility and persuasion. This is itself carries an important cultural message. Too much of the work of change theorists and the central government agencies that have pursued school reform has adopted a posture of prescriptive and messianic righteousness.

Given the complexity of the ecology of schooling, and with even a cursory reading of the history of reform efforts, this is a profoundly naïve and a-historical posture to adopt. In a way it has echoed the 'end of history' triumphalism of this millennial moment. As this triumphalism recedes on the global stage we should expect more humility to enter the discourse of school reform. *mproving Schools through Teacher Leadership* strikes just the right note here and hopefully presages a more sensitive and sensible strategy for the improvement of the educational enterprise. If there is a lesson for school reformers and improvers it is that "it's the teacher, stupid". Reforms which try to prescribe and proscribe to the teacher end up by being self-defeating. Whilst there may be some minor improvements at the less competent end of the teacher spectrum the effect on the creative vanguard of teachers is uniformly disastrous. It is this focus on teacher leadership that is so welcome in this book and if it marks a swing in the pendulum back to treating teachers with the dignity they deserve this is cause for profound celebration.

References

Harris, A. (2002) *School Improvement: what's in it for schools?* London: Falmer Press.

Harris, A., and Muijs, D., (2003) Teacher Leadership: A Review of the Literature, GTE and NUT websites.

Muijs, D., and Reynolds, D. (2000) School Effectiveness and Teacher Effectiveness: Some Preliminary Findings from the Evaluation of the Mathematics Enhancement Programme. *School Effectiveness and School Improvement,* 11 (3), 247–263.

Acknowledgements

The authors of this book have been fortunate to work together on a variety of research projects involving schools and teachers in many countries. Their work has been influenced by the insights and challenges offered by those working in schools on a daily basis. We would like to acknowledge and thank all the teachers and headteachers we work with who continue to enthuse, inform and inspire our research. We also wish to thank the Gatsby Foundation, the General Teaching Council and the National Union of Teachers for allowing us to draw upon the research sponsored and supported by them. Thanks also to Dr Judith Gunraj who collected the data. We are also grateful to Professor Christopher Day, Professor David Reynolds and Dr David Frost for allowing us to draw upon previous work to inform this book. A huge thank-you goes to Louisa Hopkins for helping us to finalise the manuscript. Finally, we'd like to thank the series editors Professor Andy Hargreaves and Professor Ivor Goodson, together with Fiona Richman from Open University Press, for their support, tolerance and patience.

Introduction

> It remains that the superhero images of leadership do not work. And it remains that mandates and incentives are not powerful enough to function as engines that will drive our efforts to improve schools. In tomorrow's world success will depend upon the ability of leaders to harness the capacity of locals, to enhance sense and meaning and to build communities of responsibility.
>
> (Fullan 1993: 4)

Across many countries, economic, social and political forces have combined to create a climate in which educational reform is expected and in which schools feel continued pressure to improve. The global drive for improved educational performance has resulted in a form of accountability that places tightly prescribed targets at the centre of systemic change. World-wide educational reform has embraced standardization as the solution to raising standards and improving economic competitiveness. As Elmore (2000: 4) notes:

> standards-based reform has a deceptively simple logic: schools and school systems should be held accountable for their contributions to pupil learning. It explicitly locates responsibility for pupil learning with the school and those who work within it, emphasizing that all pupils can learn.

While 'soulless standardization' has certainly promoted successive waves of systemic change in many countries, improved educational performance has been much more elusive (Hargreaves 2004). Part of the failure to deliver sustainable improvements in teaching and learning lies in the particular pattern of reform adopted, which is essentially one of increased accountability and restructuring as a route to school improvement. While both these approaches undoubtedly have the potential to promote changes in teaching and learning, the evidence would suggest that they rarely result in sustainable school and student improvement (Elmore 2000). Alternatively, the school improvement research evidence consistently points towards the long-term benefits to schools and students of teacher collaboration, investment in professional learning and in generating communities of practice that promote rather than stultify creativity and flexibility (Harris 2002b). The answer to improving schools, it would seem, resides in cultural rather than structural change and in the expansion rather than the reduction of teacher ingenuity and innovation.

The failure of standards-based reform to secure widespread system improvement has recently prompted a dramatic shift in educational policy in England. Following a decade or so of increased centralization, accountability and standardization, educational policy is now firmly fixed on securing school improvement through creating interdependency between schools. Currently schools are being actively encouraged to embrace new forms of cooperation and collaboration with the promise of extra resource or kudos for their efforts. The Department for Education and Skills is currently promoting collaborative networks of schools and, more specifically, supporting school partnerships in the form of 'tight' or 'loosely' coupled federations. This policy drive is viewed as one of the prime levers for securing higher achievement and improved learning outcomes.

This policy imperative not only represents a considerable shift away from the drive for hard-edged competition between schools but also places teachers, local education authorities, national agencies, researchers and schools centre stage in national reform efforts. This inevitably raises several important issues. First, there is an inherent tension and contradiction between the continued existence of the central apparatus of standardization and accountability alongside the aspiration that by collaborating schools can transfer knowledge, innovate collectively and improve teaching and learning. How can schools be encouraged to work in authentic partnerships if they are judged and assessed independently? While an emphasis upon partnership, collaboration and networking is to be welcomed, it does assume that teachers automatically possess the will, skill and ability to work in this way.

Secondly, the policy emphasis upon collaboration also assumes that all schools have the same possibility and opportunity of being part of a network, federation or partnership. For schools considered to be in challenging circumstances and/or identified as failing to meet the floor targets set by government, the collaborative playing field may be far from level. In his most recent work, Hargreaves (2004) has suggested that there is the potential for an 'apartheid of school improvement' created by the fact that schools which are performing well are given the latitude and resource to collaborate and innovate. Conversely, those schools which are considered to be under-performing are in receipt of even tighter prescription and scrutiny. The resulting effect is a sharp divide between those schools that are able to participate in the new collaborative or networking efforts and those schools that are exempt because of their under-performance. Put bluntly, those schools best placed to improve are rewarded by being given even greater opportunities to develop, change and grow. Conversely, those schools in less favourable circumstances with poorer results are penalized by the imposition of even tighter control and prescription. While there are examples of partnerships between schools in difficulty and schools in more favourable circumstances, there is little evidence to suggest that these partnerships are genuinely two-way or that there is a joint innovative process at work.

Thirdly, there is the very important question of 'networking for what purpose?' While the process of collaboration or networking is one that has been enthusiastically embraced by schools, the focus on outcomes has been less sharply focused. There is a danger that the rhetoric of networking will overshadow the need to look critically at what networks do, what they produce and whether teaching and learning improve as a result. The appeal of collaboration is particularly strong in an education system premised upon competition and control for over a decade. Consequently, there needs to be careful consideration and some systematic evaluation of whether and how far these new collaborative arrangements contribute to improved learning outcomes, for both teachers and pupils.

Finally, networking and collaboration present major challenges for the ways in which teachers understand their work, their roles and responsibilities. Working in collaboration across schools implies sharing, knowledge transfer and mutual learning. It also locates the remit for change and development across schools with teachers rather than headteachers or their senior management teams. Whether tightly or loosely configured, the net result of teachers working collaboratively across schools will be to engage them in various forms of leadership activity. Working in this way, they automatically become catalysts for change and development and take on the prime task of leading change. Within partnership arrangements, the divisions between teaching and leadership are blurred and not as clearly demarcated within individual schools. Consequently, one of the major implications of collaborative ways of working between schools is the redefinition, relocation and reconceptualization of leadership within and between schools.

School leadership

In England and many other Western countries, there has been a renewed interest in the power of leadership to generate and sustain school improvement. A premium has been placed upon the potential of school leadership to contribute to school improvement and to create the conditions in which the best teaching and learning can occur. The establishment of a National College for School Leadership (NCSL) both symbolized and reinforced a widespread belief in the ability of school leaders to deliver higher performance and system-wide transformation. It also firmly located leadership and leadership development at the centre of system renewal and change. No other country has invested so much resource (£90 million per annum) in the preparation, training and development of its school leaders. The stakes are high and the demand for improved results plus a positive impact upon schools without question.

The NCSL, quite predictably, focused its initial developmental and research efforts on headteachers. The National Qualification for Headteachers is the centerpiece of a number of programmes aimed directly at heads. However, most recently the NCSL has broadened the remit to include middle-level leaders in the shape of heads of department, subject coordinators, heads of year and key stage coordinators. These 'teacher leaders' in a formal leadership role are able to participate in a specially designed programme, Leading from the Middle, aimed at preparing those in middle-level positions for a wide range of leadership demands. However, in contrast to other countries (e.g. USA, Canada and Australia), little attention has been given to the concept of teacher leadership, in a broader sense. Indeed, the concept of teacher leadership is not one that finds a ready recognition within the English education system (Muijs and Harris 2003).

If one turns to the research literature, there is some cause for optimism that the leadership of those in formal positions of power can contribute to school and student improvement. The school effectiveness and school improvement research evidence shows quite clearly that effective leaders exert a powerful influence on the effectiveness of the school and the achievement of students (Wallace 2002). It is clear that, at best, effective leaders in the shape of headteachers exercise a significant influence on the achievement of students, but it is clear that this effect is mediated through the actions of others, particularly teachers (Leithwood and Jantzi 2000). In short, the contribution of headteacher or principal leadership to school effectiveness and school improvement is significant but not as significant as that of teacher leadership (Wallace 2002).

There is a need for caution before moving too quickly to assuming that the 'leadership equals improved student learning outcomes' equation is either linear or proven. The literature that has focused on this particular relationship is limited but consistent in that it demonstrates an indirect rather than direct relationship. This would suggest that despite the prevailing view and assumptions about leadership and school improvement, there is still much that is not yet understood about exactly how, in what form and from what origin educational leadership is able to transform schools (Leithwood and Reil 2003). There is emerging evidence about the relationship between distributed leadership and improvement, but this research base also remains limited.

In a theoretical sense, as Bush and Glover (2003) point out, there is a plethora of 'alternative and competing models of leadership' (p. 7). In their recent review of the leadership literature, Bush and Glover (2003) identify eight models of leadership that provide 'a starting point for a normative assessment of school leadership' (p. 12). They also point out the weak empirical support for these constructs and the artificial distinctions between the different models.

Looking at the leadership literature, it is difficult to discern how different theoretical positions or models of leadership differ. Although Bush and Glover (2003) argue for an 'integrated model of leadership', such a model is unlikely when there are different labels applied to the same conceptual terrain – 'instructional leadership', 'learner-centred leadership', 'pedagogical leadership'. Much more importantly, what evidence is there that these different models or constructs of leadership contribute to improved learner outcomes? As Leithwood and Reil (2003) note, 'large scale studies of schooling conclude that the effects of leadership on student learning are small but educationally significant' (p. 3).

A contemporary review of the literature (Hallinger and Heck 1996a, b) identified certain 'blank spots' (i.e. shortcomings in the research) and 'blind spots' (i.e. areas that have been overlooked because of theoretical and epistemological biases) within the leadership field. An important blank spot concerns exactly what forms of leadership practice contribute to sustained school improvement. An important blind spot is that much of the research literature has focused upon the formal leadership of headteachers in particular, and has overlooked the kinds of leadership that can be distributed across many roles and functions in the school. It has tended to be overreliant on accounts of headteachers to define effective leadership in action and, to a certain extent, neglected leadership at other levels or from other perspectives (Harris and Muijs 2003).

Although the international research base on leadership is vast, the evidential base is very diverse and the nature of studies varies considerably. As noted earlier, relatively few studies have established any direct causal links between leadership and improved student performance (Hallinger and Heck 1996a, b). While a recent systematic review of the literature confirmed that effective leadership was an important factor in a school's success, it highlighted that its effect upon student learning outcomes was largely indirect (Bell *et al.* 2003). One tentative conclusion from these findings was that distributed leadership was more likely to have an effect on the positive achievement of student outcomes than leadership that was largely, or exclusively, 'top-down'. Work by Silins and Mulford (2002) similarly suggests that student outcomes are more likely to improve where leadership sources are distributed throughout the school community and where teachers are empowered in areas of importance to them.

In their recent review of successful school improvement efforts, Glickman *et al.* (2001:49) provide a composite list of the characteristics of what they term the 'improving school', a 'school that continues to improve student learning outcomes for all students over time'. At the top of this list appears 'varied sources of leadership, including distributed leadership'. The most recent literature on change and school improvement also suggests that the form of leadership most often associated with improved learning outcomes is one that is distributed or shared (Fullan 2001; Hopkins 2001). The literature on teacher leadership (Muijs and Harris 2003) similarly reinforces the potential of distributed or diffuse forms of leadership to generate improvements in teaching and learning. Even though the conventional wisdom of leadership as role or position tends to prevail, there is a groundswell towards alternative interpretations of leadership and the beginnings of a 'paradigm shift' away from orthodox thinking about leadership practice in schools. As Day *et al.* (2000) have argued, 'the time has come to consider radical alternatives to the traditional model of leadership ... in times of rapid change and novel circumstances we need the most adaptable and flexible structures it is possible to devise' (p. 11).

The positive and negative influences of leaders upon school culture and performance have been well documented, but there remains a continuing search for a model of effective leadership that is suited to the post-modern context. For example, contemporary leadership studies have focused upon the 'moral purpose' or 'moral craft' of leadership (Sergiovanni 1994), they have considered leadership as building a 'community of learners' (Barth 1990; Senge 1990), and have viewed leadership as 'transformational' or 'liberating' (Sergiovanni 1996). However, it has become increasingly apparent that for schools to develop and improve in rapidly changing times, issues of leadership and management can no longer simply be seen as the exclusive preserve of senior staff. Successive research studies have shown that within the most effective schools, leadership extends beyond the senior management team to encompass other levels within the school (Lambert 1998; MacBeath 1998; Day *et al.* 2000; Harris 2000c).

Most recently, researchers have argued that traditional theories of leadership are no longer valid in the current reality and complexity of schooling (Sergiovanni 1996; Fullan 1999; Day *et al.* 2000). Theorists are calling for a new perspective on leadership, one that involves a decentralized, devolved and shared approach to leadership within the school (Lambert 1998; Day *et al.* 2000). Studies in the field have highlighted the importance of shared decision making, distributed leadership, constructivist leadership, value-centred leadership and emotional leadership. Writers such as Lambert (1998) and Day *et al.* (2000) have called for an examination of non-traditional perspectives on school leadership. Their work advocates the centrality of teachers in the leadership task and highlights the importance of teachers' involvement in leadership. As Ogawa and Bossert (1995) suggest, 'leadership is embedded not in particular roles but in the relationships that exist among the incumbents of roles' (p. 7).

This book

The rationale for this book resides in the increasing weight of empirical evidence that demonstrates the potential and potency of teacher leadership, which includes the leadership of support staff, both within and between schools. The growth of networking, partnerships and federations means that organizational boundaries are shifting and a redefinition of what is meant by leadership is already underway. The 'old order' of leadership equalling headship is unlikely to prevail as the architecture of schooling becomes more diverse, complex and innovative. The 'new order' is premised upon a view of leadership that is distributed and empowers those closest to the classroom to undertake leadership tasks and actions. The central argument of the book is that leadership is a fluid and emergent entity rather than a fixed phenomenon. It suggests that leadership is not simply a list of traits, skills and competencies, but the by-product of social interaction and purposeful collaboration. This inevitably implies a reconfiguration of power relationships within the school as the distinctions between followers and leaders begin to blur. It also opens up the possibility for all teaching staff to become leaders at various times and to be the creators of change, not merely the recipients.

The school improvement efforts of the last decade have pointed to the fact that something important was missing. The narrow and often piecemeal attempts to improve schools in the past have ignored the need for the fundamental supportive cultures and conditions necessary for achieving significant gains in teaching and learning. Far too often teachers have worked in their own individual classrooms lacking any productive interaction with colleagues from whom they may have gained new insights and understandings about their practice. The overarching message about successful school improvement is one of building a community of practice that offers an infrastructure to support teachers leading and learning from each other.

This book considers some of the leadership processes that contribute to building professional learning communities in schools. It does not claim to be the definitive or the last word on teacher leadership or professional learning communities, as there is important work underway in both areas. For example, a national research project funded by the Department for Education and Skills, the National College for School Leadership and the General Teaching Council for England, 'Creating and Sustaining Effective Professional Learning Communities' (http://www.eplc.info/), is currently exploring the notion of a 'professional learning community' in the UK context. The aims of the project are to identify and provide practical examples of: 'the characteristics of professional learning communities in different kinds of schools'; 'key factors inside and outside schools which seem to help or hinder the development of their professional learning communities'; 'innovative practices for ongoing professional learning and development'. In addition, recent work by Lieberman and Miller (2004) provides a contemporary insight into teacher leadership and school, teacher and student improvement.

This book consists of four parts. Part One focuses on the theoretical and conceptual background to teacher leadership. Chapter 1 considers the scope and nature of teacher leadership, exploring the roles and responsibilities associated with teachers being leaders. Chapter 2 looks at the idea of distributed leadership in some depth, drawing upon the major theoretical perspectives and highlighting the relationship between teacher leadership practice and distributed leadership theory. Chapter 3 considers the literature on school improvement and the evidence in support of teacher leadership, along with its contribution to school level change and development.

Part Two considers how teacher leadership is enhanced and developed in schools. Chapter 4 considers the important link between building professional learning communities and the role of teacher leaders. It suggests that supportive and shared leadership is most likely to generate and sustain professional learning communities. Chapter 5 explores the role of professional development in promoting teacher change and teacher learning. Chapter 6 considers the responsibility of the headteacher in generating and supporting teacher leadership. It also considers the implications for policy makers, practitioners and researchers of this alternative model of leadership operating in schools.

Part Three considers recent empirical evidence about the relationship between teacher leadership, school/teacher effectiveness and improvement from two projects. The first, the Gatsby Teacher Effectiveness Study, focuses upon the relationship between teacher leadership and teacher effectiveness. This project was conceived and designed to explore the dimensions, contours and components of effective teaching in primary and elementary mathematics. Chapter 7 draws upon the findings from this study to investigate the relationship between teacher leadership and teacher effectiveness. Chapter 8 considers differential teacher effectiveness in more depth and outlines the implications for changing roles and responsibilities for those teachers in leadership roles.

The second study, funded by the General Teaching Council for England (GTC) in conjunction with the National Union of Teachers (NUT), focused exclusively on teacher leadership as a distinctive form of professional collaboration for school improvement (Muijs and Harris 2003). Within the project, 'teacher leadership' is defined as 'the capacity for teachers to exercise leadership for teaching and learning within and beyond the classroom'. Chapter 9 provides the background to the GTC/NUT study and summarizes the research findings from the work. Chapters 10, 11 and 12 provide in-depth case study accounts of schools where teacher leadership exists to varying degrees. The main facilitators and barriers to the development of teacher leadership are discussed in each case.

Finally, Part Four considers the messages and future directions for teacher leadership. Chapter 13 summarizes the main lessons about successful teacher leadership derived from the literature and recent empirical studies. Chapter 14 concludes the book by exploring the central idea of improving schools through teacher leadership. Both the chapter and the book conclude that to really embrace 'teacher leadership' means engaging in a new professionalism that gives teachers more autonomy and self-direction. This new professionalism implies teachers reclaiming the educational ground currently under the occupation of standards-based reform, with its apparatus of testing, inspection and league tables, and leading the way in change, development and innovation. There are no easy trade-offs here, as accountability and autonomy simply do not blend well. The limitations of large-scale reform, top-down leadership and government-driven school improvement are well known. To continue with this approach to school improvement will guarantee only mediocre success and little capacity building within the system. To depart from this approach to school improvement means viewing innovation and reform as much more school- and teacher-led. This is inherently risky, as it returns professional autonomy and decision making to those in schools while simultaneously removing it from central control. However, looking back at the legacy of failed initiatives over the last decade and the inability of external reform to scale up from the few to the many, this would seem to be a risk well worth taking.

Part 1

Teacher leadership: theoretical background

one

Teacher leadership

Introduction

In the current climate, there is still much interest in and desire for sustained school improvement. We know a great deal about school improvement from the extensive research base. The messages about *how* schools improve remain fairly consistent. It is clear from the many school improvement studies that have been conducted that leadership is a key factor in a school's ability to improve. This form of leadership has often been associated with the leadership of the headteacher or principal and it has been assumed that this individual's leadership ability or skill is a critical factor in promoting school improvement, change and development. In contrast to this position, others have argued that successful school improvement is co-constructed and that leadership for school improvement is a form of 'constructivist leadership' (Lambert 1998), where leadership is primarily about learning together and constructing meaning and knowledge collectively and collaboratively. This constructivist approach to leadership creates the opportunities to surface and mediate perceptions, to inquire about and generate ideas together, to seek to reflect upon and make sense of work in the light of shared beliefs and new information, and to create actions that grow out of these new understandings. It is, in essence, teacher leadership in action.

The evidence from the school improvement literature also indicates that schools which are improving tend to be marked by a constant interchange of professional dialogue, both formally and informally. Also, they have ways of working that encourage teachers to work together towards shared goals. There is a body of evidence that demonstrates that teachers work most effectively when they are supported by other teachers and work together collegially. Hopkins *et al.* (1994) note that 'successful schools create collaborative environments which encourages involvement, professional development, mutual support and assistance in problem solving' (p. 177).

Recent assessments of the relationship between leadership and school improvement imply that giving others real responsibility and developing others is the best way for a school to move forward (Day *et al.* 2000). The evidence suggests that where this distributed form of leadership is in place, there is greater potential for building the internal capacity for change. In practice, distributed leadership means giving teachers the opportunity to lead and to take responsibility for the areas of change of most importance to the school. As will be highlighted later, this form of leadership necessarily requires relinquishing the idea of structure as control and viewing structure as the vehicle for empowering others. For this approach to work requires a high degree of trust, as trust is essential to support the leadership climate. As Evans (1998) notes: 'Trust is the essential link between leader and led, vital to people's job, status functions and loyalty, vital to fellowship. It is doubly important when organisations are reaching rapid improvement, which requires exceptional effort and competence, and doubly so again in organisations like schools that offer few motivators' (p. 183).

It is suggested therefore that the type of leadership which leads to school improvement is not one that is necessarily aligned to a formal leadership role or function, but is more of a dynamic between individuals within an organization that is a catalyst for change. In this sense, leadership is located between and among individuals within an organization; it belongs to a broad group of people, including non-teaching staff, parents and students, who all contribute to the school's distinctive culture and community. Throughout this book, the term 'teacher leadership' is deliberately intended to encapsulate *all staff* engaged in supporting teaching and learning processes, including non-teaching and support staff. This view of leadership focuses on the relationships and the connections among individuals within a school.

Although the quality of teaching strongly influences pupil motivation and achievement, it has been consistently argued that the quality of leadership matters in determining the motivation of teachers and the quality of teaching in the classroom (Fullan 2001). A preliminary glance at the leadership research literature, however, reveals that it is largely premised upon individual impetus rather than collective action and offers a singular view of leadership predominantly bound up with headship. As Murphy (2000) notes, the 'great man' theory of leadership prevails in spite of a groundswell towards leadership as empowerment, transformation and community building. This may be because schools as organizational structures remain largely unchanged, equating leadership with status, authority and position. One of the most congruent findings from recent studies of effective leadership is that authority to lead need not be located in the person of the leader but can be dispersed throughout the school, between and among people (MacBeath 1998; Day *et al.* 2000; Harris 2002b). In this sense, leadership is separated from person, role and status and is primarily concerned with the relationships and the connections among individuals within a school.

Leadership can be defined as providing vision, direction and support towards a different and preferred state – suggesting change. Thus, leadership, change and school improvement are closely related. It could be said that leaders are change-makers and don't necessarily need to reside at the top of an organization. Louis and Miles's (1990) case studies of change efforts at five secondary schools and Hord and Huling-Austin's (1986) synthesis of change and facilitation activities in nine primary schools suggest a number of things about successful school change. Louis and Miles (1990) reported that successful change leaders consistently articulated a vision for their schools so that everyone understood the vision; most importantly, they shared influence, authority, responsibility and accountability with the staff in shaping the vision so that there was shared ownership of the vision. They also engaged in formal data collection, analysis, reporting and transfer of data, for summative and formative evaluation purposes. They coordinated and orchestrated the change effort, exhibiting enormous persistence, tenacity and willingness to live with risks. Louis and Miles (1990) observed that teacher leaders required a high tolerance for complexity and ambiguity.

More recent studies have pointed to the importance of cultivating a context in which change is valued and the need to distribute leadership widely within the organization is reinforced. In the USA, Canada and Australia, the notion of 'distributed' leadership is gaining popularity. This model of leadership implies a redistribution of power and a realignment of authority within the organization. It means creating the conditions in which people work together and learn together, where they construct and refine meaning, leading to a shared purpose or set of goals. Evidence would suggest that where such conditions are in place, leadership is a much stronger internal driver for school improvement and change (Hopkins 2001). In Britain and to some extent Europe, conventional notions of leadership still tend to prevail, with an emphasis upon the leadership of those at the apex of the organization. Leadership tends to be associated with a formal role or responsibility and is generally viewed as a singular rather than a collective endeavour. A preliminary glance at the leadership research literature also reveals that leadership is largely premised upon individual impetus rather than collective action and a singular view of leadership, predominantly bound up with headship, still dominates.

As the limitations of singular or individual leadership have become increasingly evident, there has been a groundswell, particularly in the USA, Canada and Australia, towards various forms of teacher leadership. In the USA, the number of teacher leadership programmes and initiatives has grown strongly over the past decade and the notion of teacher leadership is now widely accepted by practitioners and researchers alike (Smylie 1995). Here teacher leadership is primarily concerned with enhanced leadership roles and decision-making powers for teachers. There is a sense of being on the edge of a new era of teacher professionalism, which is currently being echoed around the world; for example, in Australia in 'Developing Teacher Leaders' (Crowther *et al.* 2000) and in the UK in the Specialist Schools Trust 'Young Leaders Programme' and in the 'Teacher-led School Improvement' work undertaken by the University of Cambridge and the University of Canterbury, respectively (Frost and Durrant 2002). All of these programmes have drawn support and inspiration from a substantial body of North American work in the late 1980s and 1990s focusing on educational reform and teacher professionalism (see, for example, Lieberman 1988; Hargreaves 1991; Fullan 1993). This work suggests that teacher leadership offers a radical departure from the traditional understanding of school leadership for two reasons. First, because it equates leadership with agency, focusing upon the relationships among people and crossing organizational boundaries. Secondly, it sees leadership as not simply being about a role or function but rather as a dynamic between individuals within an organization.

Teacher leadership

The notion of teacher leadership is certainly not new. Teachers have for a long time taken the roles of team leaders, department heads, association leaders and curriculum developers. However in these roles teachers have often served as 'representatives' of change rather than 'leaders' who enact or initiate change. Recently, research on school development and change has led to strong and compelling pleas for dramatically different roles for teachers, including increased leadership roles. Such work emphasizes the need for teachers to extend their sphere of influence beyond the classroom and into school-wide leadership activities. This advocacy for teacher professionalism and expanded leadership roles is premised on the belief that as they are closest to the classroom, teachers can implement changes that make a difference to learning and learners.

Studies have also shown that teachers do not subscribe to traditional definitions of leadership as 'higher' or 'superior' positions within the organizational hierarchy. Instead, teachers view leadership as a collaborative effort, a 'banding together' with other teachers to promote professional development and growth and the improvement of educational services (Troen and Boles 1992). Today, through initiatives such as 'Networked Learning Communities', leadership roles have begun to emerge with real opportunities for teachers to impact upon educational change, without necessarily leaving the classroom. Teachers are now serving as research colleagues, working as advisor-mentors to new teachers, and facilitating professional development activities. They are also acting as members of school-based leadership teams and leaders of change efforts.

But what exactly is meant by teacher leadership? In essence, teacher leadership is a model of leadership in which teaching staff at various levels within the organization have the opportunity to lead (Harris and Lambert 2003). This model of leadership means creating the conditions in which people work together and learn together, where they construct and refine meaning, leading to a shared purpose or set of goals. Teacher leadership is conceptualized as a set of behaviours and practices that are undertaken collectively. It is primarily concerned with the relationships and connections among individuals within a school. A key element in the model of leadership proposed is that the nature and purpose of leadership is 'the ability of those within a school to work together, constructing meaning and knowledge collectively and collaboratively' (Lambert 1998: 5). Taking this stance, leadership is a fluid and emergent rather than a fixed phenomenon (Gronn 2000: 324). As Wheatley (2000) notes: 'We have known for nearly half a century that self-managed teams are far more productive than any other forms of organising. There is a clear correlation between participation and productivity. There is both a desire to participate more and strong evidence that such participation leads to the effectiveness and productivity we crave' (p. 2).

Teacher leadership has implications for the division of labour within a school, particularly when the tasks facing the organization are shared more widely. It also opens up the possibility of all teachers becoming leaders at various times. It is this last dimension that has most potency and potential for school improvement because it is premised upon collaborative forms of working among teachers.

Wenger's (1998) notion of 'communities of practice' is also particularly helpful in understanding collaborative ways of working in schools. It suggests that individuals derive their understanding of their work from the community of practice within which they carry it out. The members of the community have a shared understanding of the work and individuals are drawn into the community by a process of learning where the boundaries are that define the collection of tasks which make up the practice. There are two important points about communities of practice. First, everyone is a member of more than one community of practice. Teachers, for example, are part of a wider community of teachers, which defines certain aspects of behaviour as legitimate, while also being members of a school. Secondly, teachers are simultaneously members of a school, of a subject area and an individual classroom. Through this multiple membership, individuals transact the expectations of one community of practice into others.

Wenger (1998) suggests that individuals derive their identity from their membership of, and participation in, communities of practice. He suggests that 'communities of practice become resources for organising our learning as well as contexts in which to manifest our learning through an identity of participation' (p. 273). Hence, a learning community involves multiple forms of membership and participation. Consequently, to view leadership as a collective activity offers greater opportunity for organizational development, change and improvement (Harris 2001).

The terms 'teacher leaders' and 'teacher leadership' appear in the literature in a variety of contexts (see Harris and Muijs 2003). Katzenmeyer and Moller (2001), for example, define them in the following way: 'teachers who are leaders lead within and beyond the classroom, identify with and contribute to a community of teacher learners and leaders, and influence others towards improved educational practice' (p. 5). Note, however, that they begin with 'teachers who are leaders', which suggests that certain teachers are selected to undertake designated leadership roles; this is only one of a number of possible interpretations of the idea of course. At this stage, a rough hewn typology may be suggested. In some cases, a specific 'teacher leader' role is assumed; in others, the expectation is that teachers who already occupy a formal management position (middle managers) will be the ones to exercise leadership. A further category is one which includes a range of distinct professional development and research roles. Another category is simply leadership exercised by teachers regardless of position or designation. These categories are discussed in some detail below.

Lead teachers

Lead teachers are those teachers who have been appointed to 'teacher leader' roles for specific purposes. In both the USA and England, national reform initiatives have increasingly focused on 'the classroom level', which has led to the appointment of experienced practitioners to posts dedicated to improving colleagues' performance. The work of these external change agents might include organizational diagnosis and building collaborative relationships in schools (Little 1990). The term 'lead teachers' is also used to describe a form of coaching that involves classroom observation. Little (1990) talks of 'school-level instructional leadership teams' in which the 'lead teachers' still retain a 60 per cent teaching commitment but the rest of the time is spent observing teaching and giving feedback to teachers. For Lieberman (1988), the role of the 'teacher leader' is part of 'the second wave of school reform', which implies a thrust from the outside in.

More recently in England, a large number of expert classroom practitioners have been recruited by local education authorities (LEAs) to act as teaching and learning consultants with a specific brief to implement the Key Stage 3 Strategy. The 'advanced skills teacher' designation is another Department for Education and Skills (DfES) scheme in which schools can appoint or designate expert practitioners who then act as consultants for a proportion of their time. This development echoes the extensive appointment by LEAs of advisory teachers or what, in the 1980s, Biott and colleagues called 'semi-detached teachers' (Biott 1991). One of the contributors to Biott's book described himself as a 'support teacher' and associated himself with the American literature on teacher leadership.

Subject leaders

It is increasingly the case that heads of departments, subject leaders and subject coordinators are expected to exercise leadership. Since 1998, there has been a radical shift in the role and responsibilities of curriculum subject and departmental leaders. The Subject Leader Standards represent a major redefinition of the role, expectations and performance of leaders at departmental and subject level. The standards highlight the importance of high-quality teaching and improved standards of achievement (Teacher Training Agency 1998). They also acknowledge the importance of 'establishing high standards of teaching and learning in their subject as well as playing a major role in the development of school policy' (p. 3).

Team leaders have a powerful influence over classroom practices and are important gatekeepers to change and development within their subject areas. The Subject Leader Standards acknowledge the centrality of the subject leader in contributing to whole-school policy and development. The overall purpose of the subject leader's role is to contribute to school improvement and increased standards of performance through the provision of high-quality teaching within the subject area. To achieve this, the subject leader has to lead and manage the curriculum and to respond to the internal and external demands for accountability and quality. All of these demands have to be met in the particular context of the individual school and the community it serves.

Within a school the skills, abilities and expertise of subject leaders will inevitably vary. Differences exist between departments in terms of performance and effectiveness. However, it is possible to develop and improve leadership at this level through the provision of structured support. It has been shown that an optimum source of support resides in other subject leaders or heads of department within the school. By drawing upon the expertise and knowledge of those in middle management positions in the same context, the possibility of improvement across departments is significantly enhanced.

Consequently, the scope and role of subject leaders has been extended quite dramatically. Subject and departmental leaders are now responsible for formulating and implementing policies for the subject or area of work, for devising short-, medium- and long-term plans, for setting challenging targets, for promoting effective practice; and for reviewing progress. These activities involve all the staff who contribute to the subject area and will relate directly to the school's vision, policies, priorities and targets. Most importantly, subject and departmental leaders are responsible for ensuring that the teaching within the subject area is effective; that teaching is regularly and systematically monitored and evaluated; that student targets are set; and that resources are used efficiently.

While subject and departmental leaders are very much in the front line, this does not necessarily mean that they are automatically involved in school-level decision making. Levels of involvement vary according to the management approach of senior staff and the way in which both groups interact. To contribute to whole-school development, subject and departmental leaders need to be participants in policy development and strategic planning. This requires structural change, where a formal 'two-way' equal relationship is established between middle and senior management. It also requires cultural change, where subject or departmental leaders are integrally involved in decision making and policy developments within the school. As team leaders, their role is to foster trust and mutual support within the team. Consequently, the challenge facing subject and departmental leaders is how to foster a climate of change and innovation that leads to improved learning outcomes for students

Coordinators

Coordinators are teachers who have been designated as mentors, coordinators of continuing professional development, special educational needs Coordinators (SENCOs) and facilitators of action research. There are a variety of roles in which teachers are called upon to support the professional learning of their colleagues. These include the induction and mentoring of teachers new to the school and the coordination of continuing professional development activities. In a minority of schools in England, some teachers are designated as 'research coordinator', a role aimed at facilitating action research. The Networked Learning Communities Initiative has led to the development not only of research capacity in the participating schools, but also to the development of the role of 'school research coordinator'. There are questions, however, about the extent to which teachers may be reluctant to become involved in data-gathering activities in each others' classrooms, seen by some to be intrusive and too closely allied with inspection and performance management.

Informal teacher leadership

Informal teacher leadership refers to the exercise of leadership by teachers regardless of position or designation. This has also been referred to as 'invisible leadership' (Bascia 1997). This is a feature of a particular strand of research and development in the UK that has sought to distinguish itself by emphasizing the capacity of all teachers to engage in 'teacher-led development work' (Frost and Durrant 2002). The model of support that Frost and Durrant promote depends on partnerships with external agents rather than externally derived initiatives. For them:

> It is not a matter of delegation, direction or distribution of responsibility, but rather a matter of teachers' agency and their choice in initiating and sustaining change ... Negotiation of personal development plans with colleagues ensures that they are appropriate and realistic and that the development work is likely to be supported. Systematic inquiry and classroom experimentation are key elements of the development process, evidence being used strategically to improve learning and teaching and to build capacity through collaborative development work.
>
> (Frost and Durrant 2002: 3)

It may be argued that this category ought properly to be labelled 'informal leadership':

> Teachers exercise informal leadership ... by sharing their expertise, volunteering for new projects and bringing new ideas to the school ... by helping their colleagues to carry out their classroom duties, and by assisting in the improvement of classroom practice through the engagement of their colleagues in experimentation and the examination of more powerful instructional techniques. Teachers attribute leadership qualities, as well, to colleagues who accept responsibility for their own professional growth, promote the school's mission, and work for the improvement of the school or school system.
>
> (Leithwood *et al.* 1999: 117)

The use of the term 'informal' in this context could be taken to mean simply the absence of a formal position, but it is important to preserve the distinction between activity that might be described as leadership by others and activity that is planned and exercised deliberately by teachers. The defining characteristic being that the teacher has chosen to act strategically to contribute to school improvement (Frost and Durrant 2002).

As highlighted earlier, a particularly significant shift in the school improvement field in the last few years has been the burgeoning of network or collaborative initiatives premised upon teachers leading innovation and change. Hargreaves (2004: 9) suggests that:

> A network increases the pool of ideas on which any member can draw and as one idea or practice is transferred, the inevitable process of adaptation and adjustment to different conditions is rich in potential for the practice to be incrementally improved by the recipient and then fed back to the donor in a virtuous circle of innovation and improvement. In other words, the networks extend and enlarge the communities of practice with enormous potential benefits.

At the present time there are over fifteen national policy networks or other collaboratives, plus many other local networks, often set up between universities, LEAs and schools. Some have been established with a particular focus on improving the achievement of pupils in schools in more challenging areas, some deliberately attempt to bridge the gap between schools in very different circumstances (for example, schools in deprived areas with those in much more affluent areas), and some take as part of their remit an attempt to have primary (elementary) and secondary schools work more more closely together, thus facilitating better transfer.

Many of these networks are based upon a model of teacher enquiry and teacher leadership. As such, they highlight the significantly increasing involvement of practitioners in research and evidence-based activity. In this sense, they are based on an assumption that external research cannot provide all of the answers to complex questions of school improvement. This suggests that many of the answers reside within teachers and school leaders, and collaborative enquiry and developing more effective means of sharing and developing new knowledge between schools is central to sustainable school improvement and, indeed, system-wide transformation.

The Networked Learning Communities Initiative (Jackson 2000) involves clusters of schools working in partnership with others to enhance the quality of learning at six levels: pupil; teacher; leadership; the school as a professional learning community; school-to-school; and, within this initiative, network to network. In placing teachers, leaders and schools at the heart of innovation and knowledge creation and using an enquiry model, it attempts to enable the development of local, context-specific practices and solutions that can be explained and interpreted by schools in other contexts. It also reinforces the centrality of teachers as leaders of innovation and development.

Roles and responsibilities

Several authors have provided definitions of teacher leadership that clearly delineate the differences with traditional leadership approaches. For example, Wasley (1991) defines teacher leadership as 'the ability to encourage colleagues to change, to do things they wouldn't ordinarily consider without the influence of the leader' (p. 32). In contrast to traditional notions of leadership, teacher leadership is characterized by a form of collective leadership in which teachers develop expertise by working collaboratively (Boles and Troen 1994).

A number of different roles have been suggested for teacher leaders that further explain the distinctive nature of the leadership activity. Katzenmeyer and Moller (2001) see teacher leadership as having three main facets:

- *Leadership of students or other teachers*: facilitator, coach, mentor, trainer, curriculum specialist, creating new approaches, leading study groups.
- *Leadership of operational tasks*: keeping the school organized and moving towards its goals, through roles as head of department, action researcher, member of task forces.
- *Leadership through decision making or partnership*: member of school improvement teams, member of committees, instigator of partnerships with business, higher education institutions, LEAs and parent–teacher associations.

Gehrke (1991) identifies quite similar functions of teacher leaders:

- continuously improving their own classroom teaching;
- organizing and leading reviews of school practice;
- providing curriculum development knowledge;
- participating in in-school decision making;
- giving in-service training to colleagues; and
- participating in the performance evaluation of teachers.

Harris (2002a) suggests that there are four discernible and discrete dimensions of the teacher leadership role. The first dimension concerns the way in which teachers translate the principles of school improvement into the practices of individual classrooms. This *brokering* role remains a central responsibility for the teacher as leader. It ensures that links within schools are secure and that opportunities for meaningful development among teachers are maximized. A second dimension of the teacher leader role focuses upon *participative* leadership where all teachers feel part of the change or development and have a sense of ownership. Teacher leaders may assist other teachers to cohere around a particular development and to foster a more collaborative way of working (Blase and Anderson 1995). They work with colleagues to shape school improvement efforts and take some lead in guiding teachers towards a collective goal. A third dimension of teacher leadership in school improvement is the *mediating* role. Teacher leaders are important sources of expertise and information. They are able to draw critically upon additional resources and expertise if required and to seek external assistance. Finally, a fourth and possibly the most important dimension of the teacher leadership role is *forging close relationships* with individual teachers through which mutual learning takes place.

Other writers have identified further dimensions of the teacher leadership role, such as undertaking action research (Ash and Persall 2000), instigating peer classroom observation (Little 2000), or contributing to the establishment of a collaborative culture in the school (Lieberman *et al.* 2000). Of these roles, those of mentoring, induction and continual professional development of colleagues are considered crucial (Sherrill 1999), as is developing collaborative relationships with colleagues that allow new ideas and leadership to spread and impact on the school as a whole (Little 2000).

Teacher leadership roles have been identified as curriculum developers, bid writers, leaders of a school improvement team, mentors of new or less experienced staff, and action researchers with a strong link to the classroom. The important point emanating from the literature is that teacher leaders are, in the first place, expert teachers, who spend most of their time in the classroom but take on different leadership roles at different times, following the principles of formative leadership (Ash and Persall 2000). The literature asserts that the principal reason for this is to transform schools into professional learning communities (Katzenmeyer and Moller 2001) and to empower teachers to become involved closely in decision making within the school, thus contributing to the democratization of schools (Gehrke 1991). Teacher leaders should be able to work collaboratively with peers, observing one another's lessons and discussing pedagogy.

Barth (1999) sees teacher leadership extending beyond just collaborating or participating in decision making. He views teacher leadership as fulfilling some of the functions possibly undertaken by senior management, including:

- choosing textbooks and instructional materials;
- shaping the curriculum;
- setting standards for pupil behaviour;
- deciding on tracking;

- designing staff development programmes;
- setting promotion and retention policies;
- deciding school budgets;
- evaluating teacher performance;
- selecting new teachers; and
- selecting new administrators.

In this model, teacher leaders play a major role in running the school and in taking major decisions. Most other writers in the field, however, view teacher leaders as collaborators with senior management in decision making on specific aspects of school policy rather than replacing them (Gehrke 1991).

In one of the most extensive studies on the work of teacher leaders, Lieberman *et al.* (2000) focused on what teachers actually did when they assumed leadership positions designed to provide assistance to other teachers. The authors found that the work of lead teachers was varied and largely specific to the individual context of the school. To be effective with their colleagues, lead teachers found it necessary to learn a variety of leadership skills while on the job, including:

- building trust and developing rapport;
- diagnosing organizational conditions;
- dealing with processes;
- managing the work; and
- building skills and confidence in others.

The authors concluded that restructuring school communities to incorporate leadership positions for teachers necessitated teacher leaders taking certain actions. These included: placing a non-judgmental value on providing assistance, modelling collegiality as a mode of work, enhancing teachers' self-esteem, using different approaches to assistance, making provisions for continuous learning and support for teachers at the school site, and encouraging others to provide leadership to their peers.

Some studies have shown that leadership positions can yield significant personal benefits to those involved. Intellectual and professional growth and decreased isolation are personal gains reported by teachers from their new leadership roles. Teachers have also reported that their knowledge and skills in teaching increased dramatically as a result of their involvement in leadership positions (Troen and Boles 1992). New skills and knowledge also lead to increased confidence among lead teachers and a stronger commitment to teaching. It has been shown that under certain conditions lead teachers can be successful in facilitating cooperation and collegiality more broadly among faculty members, thereby decreasing the isolation many teachers experience (Hart 1995).

Research also suggests that problems often arise when teacher leadership roles are not well defined (Hart 1995). When the responsibilities that come with leadership are not well delineated, confusion results and tensions mount, not only for lead teachers but also for those who work with them (i.e. administrators, classroom teachers). At the same time, however, researchers point to the need for lead teachers to participate in the definition and creation of their new roles. Teacher leaders who are given the opportunity to create and shape their own roles receive more support and experience greater success than those who are less willing and able to take the initiative.

In summary, there are several important things to highlight about teacher leadership. First, teacher leadership is leadership as a distributed entity that requires the creation of collegial norms among teachers that research has shown contributes to school effectiveness, improvement and development. Secondly, teacher leadership means giving teachers opportunities to lead, which research shows has a positive influence upon the quality of relationships and teaching within the school. Thirdly, at its most practical, teacher leadership allows teachers to work together and provides them with a legitimate source of authority. Finally, teacher leadership challenges many current assumptions about the nature of leadership, the community within which it occurs and the relationships between power, authority and influence. In summary, it involves 'seeing leadership as the outcome of the dynamics of interpersonal relationships (an emergent property of the group) rather than just individual action' (Bennett *et al.* 2003: 6). It is leadership that is distributed to the many rather than the few. Chapter 2 discusses distributed leadership as the main theoretical framework for teacher leadership.

two

Distributed leadership

Introduction

There is a growing body of evidence within the school improvement field that points towards the importance of capacity building as a means of sustaining improvement (e.g. Mitchell and Sackney 2001; Hopkins and Jackson 2003). At the core of the capacity-building model, it has been argued, is 'distributed leadership along with social cohesion and trust' (Hopkins and Jackson 2003: 95). Leadership, from this perspective, resides in the human potential available to be released within an organization; it is what Gronn (2000) terms 'an emergent property of a group or network of individuals in which group members pool their expertise' (Bennett *et al.* 2003: 3).

Implicit within this model of distributed leadership are the leadership practices of teachers, either as informal leaders or in a formal leadership role as a head of department, subject coordinator or teacher mentor (Harris and Muijs 2003). As Leithwood and Reil (2003) note, 'research suggests that teacher leaders can help other teachers to embrace goals, to understand the changes that are needed to strengthen teaching and learning and to work towards improvement' (p. 3). The clear implication is that distributed leadership is most likely to contribute to school improvement and to build internal capacity for development.

The literature is less clear, however, on the exact form that this distributed leadership takes. Bennett *et al.* (2003) note in their recent review of the literature on distributed leadership that 'there were almost no empirical studies of distributed leadership in action' (p. 4). Hence accounts of distributed leadership in practice are not readily available and 'operational images' of distributed leadership are not forthcoming (Hopkins and Jackson 2003). While work by Spillane *et al.*, (2001b) and Harris and Muijs (2003) has started to explore distributed leadership in action, many more studies are required before firm conclusions can be drawn about the forms of distributed leadership activity that contribute to school improvement.

Distributed leadership has become increasingly used in the discourse about school leadership in the last few years and is currently receiving much attention and growing empirical support (Gronn 2000; Spillaine *et al.* 2001b; Harris 2002b; Hopkins and Jackson 2003). However, as Bennett *et al.* (2003: 2) point out, there seems to be 'little agreement as to the meaning of the term' and interpretations and understandings vary. Most helpfully, Bennett *et al.* suggest that it is best to think of distributed leadership as 'a way of thinking about leadership' rather than as another technique or practice. In understanding distributed leadership this way, it inevitably challenges assumptions about the nature and scope of leadership activity as it reconceptualizes leadership in terms of the leadership of the 'many rather than the few' (Harris and Lambert 2003: 4). Distributed leadership concentrates on engaging expertise wherever it exists within the organization rather than seeking this only through formal position or role.

In contrast to traditional notions of leadership premised upon an individual managing hierarchical systems and structures, distributed leadership is characterized as a form of collective leadership in which teachers develop expertise by working together. This distributed view of leadership, it has been suggested, offers a framework for studying leadership practice in which 'every person at entry level ... in one way or another, acts as a leader' (Goleman 2002: 14). As Elmore (2000) points out, in a 'knowledge-intensive enterprise like teaching and learning there is no way to perform these complex tasks without widely distributing the responsibility for leadership among roles in the organisation' (p. 14).

This is not to suggest that ultimately no-one is responsible for the overall performance of the organization or to render those in formal leadership roles redundant. Rather, the job of those in formal leadership positions is primarily to hold the pieces of the organization together in a productive relationship. Their central task is to create a common culture of expectations around the use of individual skills and abilities. In short, distributing leadership equates with maximizing the human capacity within the organization. The distributed perspective focuses on *how* leadership practice is distributed among formal and informal leaders. As Bennett *et al.* (2003) note, 'distributed leadership is not something "done" by an individual "to others" ... rather it is [an] emergent property of a group or network of individuals in which group members pool their expertise' (p. 3). In this sense, distributed leadership is a form of collective agency incorporating the activities of many individuals in a school who work to mobilize and guide other teachers in the process of instructional change (Spillaine *et al.* 2001a).

Distributed leadership extends the boundaries of leadership significantly as it is premised upon high levels of 'teacher involvement and decision making. It encompasses a wide variety of expertise, skill and input in the process and practice of leadership' (Harris and Lambert 2003: 16). Engaging many people in leadership activity is at the core of distributed leadership in action. Hopkins and Jackson (2003) suggest it is where 'leadership and organisational growth collide and by definition, it is dispersed or distributed' (p. 99). This implies a changing view of structures away from command and control. It suggests a view of the school as a learning community chiefly concerned with maximizing the achievement capacities of all those within the organization (Gronn 2000).

A variety of studies have also found clear evidence of the positive effect of distributed leadership on teachers' self-efficacy and morale (Greenleaf 1996; MacBeath 1998; Mitchell and Sackney 2001). Evidence suggests that where teachers share good practice and learn together, the possibility of securing better quality teaching is increased (Little 1990, 2000). Such collaboration and collegiality are at the core of distributed leadership, but it is important to recognize that distributed leadership is distinctive from, and more than, mutual collaboration between teachers. Spillane *et al.* (2001b) argue that distributed leadership 'emerges through interaction with other people and the environment' (p. 10).

The important delineation between forms of team-working, collegiality, collaboration and distributed leadership is that distributed leadership results from the activity, that it is a product of a conjoint activity such as network learning communities, study groups, inquiry partnerships and not simply another label for that activity. Not all collaborative activities will necessarily generate distributed leadership, as much depends on the level and quality of involvement plus the degree of skilfulness within the group (Harris and Lambert 2003). It also depends on the extent to which group members' activities impact upon organizational change and development. Much also depends on the internal conditions set – often by the formal leadership – to support and nurture collaborative learning and to harness the leadership energy that results.

Hopkins and Jackson (2003) suggest that formal leaders in schools need to orchestrate and nurture the space for distributed leadership to occur and to create the 'shelter conditions' for the leadership of collaborative learning. This raises the question of whether distributed leadership is 'top-down' or 'bottom-up'. Is it a form of leadership which acknowledges and depends upon the formal leadership positions within the organization, or is it more likely to occur organically and spontaneously from the activities of teachers working together? Bennett *et al.* (2003) consider the relationship between positional and informal leadership as a means of exploring the 'top-down/

bottom-up' dichotomy. They also look at sources of change and suggest that the impetus for developing distributed leadership can arise from a variety of influences and that it is possible that the 'development of a distributed leadership . . . may be found in the shape of a "top-down" initiative from a strong or charismatic leader' (p. 9). Several studies that identified the headteacher as a source or impetus for generating distributed forms of leadership are cited in their review of the literature (e.g. Gold *et al.* 2002). Other research work has similarly pointed to the role of the headteacher in fostering and generating distributed leadership and has provided illuminative rather than conclusive evidence of a relationship between school improvement and distributed leadership (Day *et al.* 2000; Harris and Chapman 2002).

Distributed leadership: theoretical perspectives

The concept of distributed leadership is far from new. As long ago as the late 1950s the possibility of leadership displaying a distributed pattern or configuration was posed in the first edition of the *Handbook of Social Psychology* (Gibb 1954). In the 1970s, this idea was revisited by organizational theorists and researchers who paid increased attention to models of situated cognition and the inherent patterns of distribution this theory implied. Their work highlighted the difficulty of separating action from the context of action, suggesting instead that the situation is critical in constituting leadership practice. This view of 'distributed leadership' assigns a central role to the relationship between agency and structure, where structure is the medium of human interaction. It implies that to understand the human situation requires an exploration of how structure and agency interact together to construct practice, including leadership practice.

In theoretical terms, the most robust and extensive contemporary analysis of distributed leadership can be found within the work of Spillane *et al.* (2001b) and Gronn (2003). Both adopt a social theory perspective on leadership, with Gronn (2003) clearly viewing activity theory as the centrepiece of his analysis. He proposes a theory of action based on the idea of conjoint agency and a consideration of Engeström's (1999) activity theory. In activity theory, the notion of activity bridges the gap between agency and structure. In Giddens' sociological theory of action, social or organizational structures can be modified by the agency of individuals by using whatever power resources are to hand (Giddens 1984). In activity theory, leadership is more of a collective phenomenon. As Gronn (2000) puts it: 'the potential for leadership is present in the flow of activities in which a set of organisation members find themselves enmeshed' (p. 331).

Explanations based on activity theory are especially applicable to professional contexts such as schools because most conceptions of professionalism include the idea of autonomous judgement. Again Gronn is helpful when he says that:

> In activities in which there is greater scope for discretion, examples of reciprocally expressed influence abound. In the relations between organisational heads and their immediate subordinates or between executives and their personal assistants for example, couplings form in which the extent of the conjoint agency resulting from the interdependence and mutual influence of the two parties is sufficient to render meaningless any assumptions about leadership being embodied in just one individual.
>
> (Gronn 2000: 331)

Gronn (2000) suggests that distributed leadership is an emergent property of a group or a network of interacting individuals. In Gronn's view, leadership is a form of concerted action which is about the additional dynamic that occurs when people work together or that is the product of conjoint agency.

Spillane *et al.* (2001b) similarly imply a way of understanding leadership that focuses upon interaction and the exploration of complex social processes. In this sense, leadership is best understood as 'practice distributed over leaders, followers and their situation'. A distributed view of leadership 'incorporates the activities of multiple groups of individuals in a school who work at guiding and mobilizing staff in the instructional change process' (p. 20). It implies a social distribution of leadership where the leadership function is *stretched over* the work of a number of individuals and where the leadership task is accomplished through the interaction of *multiple leaders* (Spillane 2001a). It implies interdependency rather than dependency, embracing how leaders of various kinds and in various roles share responsibility.

In theoretical terms therefore, distributed leadership means multiple sources of guidance and direction, following the contours of expertise in an organization, made coherent through a common culture. It is 'the "glue" of a common task or goal – improvement of instruction – and a common frame of values for how to approach that task' (Elmore 2000: 15). The distributed perspective focuses on *how* leadership practice is distributed among formal and informal leaders.

Sergiovanni's (2001) concept of leadership density is one that overlaps here. He argues that high leadership density means that a larger number of people are involved in the work of others, are trusted with information, are involved in decision making, are exposed to new ideas and are participating in knowledge creation and transfer. In such circumstances, a larger number of members of the organization have a stake in the success of the school.

Similarly, the idea of distributed leadership resonates considerably with the idea of teachers as leaders or 'teacher leadership' which is gaining some currency with researchers and practitioners across many countries (Little 2000; Muijs and Harris, 2003).

Recently, Woods (2004) has argued that there are some similarities between distributed leadership and democratic leadership but warns that democratic leadership may be eclipsed or colonized by discourses on distributed leadership. In their desk study, Bennett *et al.* (2003) talk about 'distributed or devolved leadership', while Kets de Vries (1990) defines distributed leadership in terms of effective team working linked to social activity theory. It is clear that a wide range of competing interpretations of distributed leadership theory already exist and currently feature within contemporary writing and research. As the concept becomes more popular, there is an inherent danger that it will serve as a 'catch-all' phrase to describe a wide range of loosely coupled activities without any recourse to its theoretical lineage. Consequently, the next section explores different interpretations of the term and provides an analysis of the inherent limitations of the theory to practical application.

The main point to note here is that distributed leadership, as construed by leading researchers, does not have an extensive empirical base. It is primarily a way of analysing leadership practice in schools rather than describing it. For both Spillane *et al.* (2001b) and Gronn (2000) distributed leadership is a purely analytical tool, but for other researchers working from a different empirical base it offers a framework for describing particular forms of leadership practice. The many empirical studies of 'teacher leadership' (Muijs and Harris 2003) inherently point towards the idea of distributed forms of power and authority. Yet, interestingly, despite the enthusiasm for distributed leadership within the research community, the obvious exploration of teachers as leaders within this distributed model of leadership practice is not fully embraced (Harris 2003). Similarly, the school improvement field is replete with examples of distributed forms of leadership in a very practical sense, with responsibility for organizational development and change being channelled through the many rather than the few. Again, this empirical base is largely ignored in discussions of distributed leadership or in contemporary analyses of the phenomenon (Bennett *et al.* 2003).

This fissure between theory and practice is both interesting and disturbing. On the one hand there is great enthusiasm for a theoretical perspective on the concept, as evidenced in the numerous references to Spillane *et al.* and Gronn, but on the other a general reluctance to consider the wide range of empirical evidence that has highlighted the relationship between distributed forms of leadership and improved organizational outcomes. Despite Bennett and co-workers' (2003) claim that the concept of distributed leadership is in its 'infancy', there is a large swathe of teacher leadership literature that points to the very opposite. Yet, this literature is generally factored out of the current analysis and exploration.

One reason for this may lie in a distinction between distributed leadership as perceived within a traditional organizational theory framework and distributed leadership as a process of thinking and acting in a particular situation. This distinction is one that is clearly apparent in contemporary discussions of distributed leadership. The empirical work looks for ways of describing leadership practice in action; the theoretical says very little about the nature of practice but is more concerned with capturing and interrogating the process of interaction. Hence, part of the problem in understanding exactly what is meant by distributed leadership is the blurring of two distinctly different perspectives on the term – one wholly applied and the other purely theoretical.

Woods (2004) presents a comparison between distributed forms of leadership and democratic leadership and he talks about distributed leadership as 'empowering the many eyes, ears, and brains of the organisation'. This would seem to be a very practical and applied way of understanding the term, yet most of his subsequent analysis takes a purely theoretical position to argue how democratic leadership is a superior form of distributed leadership or dispersed leadership. This is a good illustration of how the discourse about distributed leadership is predominantly theoretical but some core assumptions are being made about its practical application.

Distributed leadership: blocks and barriers

While the research evidence from the leadership and school improvement fields highlight the advantages of distributed forms of leadership, there are inevitable and inherent difficulties associated with its widespread adoption and adaptation within schools. It would be naïve to ignore the major structural, cultural and micro-political barriers operating in schools that make distributed forms of leadership difficult to implement. Clearly schools as traditional hierarchies with the demarcations of position and pay-scale are not going to be instantly responsive to a more fluid and distributed approach to leadership. Furthermore, there are inherent threats to status and the *status quo* in all that distributed leadership implies. First, distributed leadership requires those in formal leadership positions to relinquish power to others. Apart from the challenge to authority and ego, this potentially places the head or principal in a vulnerable position because of the lack of direct control over certain activities. In addition, there are financial barriers, as formal leadership positions in schools carry additional increments. Consequently, to secure informal leadership in schools will require heads to use other incentives and to seek alternative ways of remunerating staff who take on leadership responsibilities.

Secondly, the 'top-down' approaches to leadership and the internal school structures offer significant impediments to the development of distributed leadership. The current hierarchy of leadership within both primary and secondary schools means that power resides with the leadership team – that is, at the top of the school. In addition, the separate pastoral and academic structures in schools, the subject or department divisions plus the strong year groupings present significant barriers to teachers working together. These structures can actively prevent teachers attaining autonomy and taking on leadership roles within the school as they demarcate role and responsibility.

Finally, and most importantly, distributed leadership poses the major challenge of *how* to distribute development responsibility and more importantly *who* distributes responsibility and authority? It is clear that a 'top-down' approach to distributed leadership is possible and that giving improvement or development responsibilities to teachers offers a means of empowering others to lead. But it will be important to ensure that distributed leadership is not simply misguided delegation. Instead, it implies a social distribution of leadership where the leadership function is 'stretched over' the work of several individuals and where the leadership task is accomplished through the interaction *of multiple* leaders (Spillane *et al.* 2001b: 20). It implies interdependency rather than dependency, embracing the ways in which leaders of various kinds and in various roles share responsibility. As Bennett *et al.* (2003: 10) highlight, there may be both 'institutional and spontaneous' forms of distributed leadership. There may be a long-term institutional form of distributed leadership through team structures or working groups and there may be *ad hoc* groups offering a more fluid and immediate response to the change and development needs of the school. As has been demonstrated, there will inevitably be a relationship between those in formal leadership positions and those who are involved in leadership and development activities at other levels. It is clear that certain tasks and functions would have to be retained by those in formal leadership positions but that the key to successful distributed leadership resides in the involvement of teachers in collectively guiding and shaping instructional and institutional development.

Under the right conditions, the positive benefits of distributed leadership have clearly been shown. King (1996) and Griffin (1995) found that distributed leadership resulted in positive effects on pedagogy, on school culture and on educational quality. However, the research also points towards the importance of allocating time for teachers to work together and generate developmental activity of benefit to the school. In her study of a school where distributed leadership was being implemented, Ovando (1994) found that time to meet was a central component of success and that in schools that were improving, teachers were given dedicated time to collaborate with one another.

The research evidence would also suggest that the success or otherwise of distributed leadership within a school can be influenced by a number of interpersonal factors, such as relationships with other teachers and school management. The importance of these is evident, both with respect to teachers' ability to influence colleagues and with respect to developing productive relations with school management, who may in some cases feel threatened by teachers taking on leadership roles. There may also be conflicts between groups of teachers, such as those that do and do not take on leadership roles, which can lead to estrangement among teachers. Research has shown that colleagues can at times be hostile to distributed leadership because of inertia, over-cautiousness and insecurity (Barth 1999). Overcoming these difficulties will require a combination of strong interpersonal skills on the part of the 'teacher leader' and a school culture that encourages change and leadership from teachers.

The evidence presented in this chapter suggests that successful leaders are those who distribute leadership, understand relationships and recognize the importance of 'reciprocal learning processes that lead to shared purposes' (Harris and Lambert 2003: 7). Essentially, these leaders are more connected to people and networks than the 'traditional' forms of leadership – that is, 'the lone chief atop a pyramidal structure' (Greenleaf 1996: 61); they distribute leadership to generate organizational development and change. Yet, as Hopkins and Jackson (2003) note, 'despite more than two decades of writing about organisational development we are still in a position of needing to develop understandings about what leadership really involves when it is distributed, how schools might function and act differently and what operational images of distributed leadership in action might look like' (p. 17). In addition, despite a wealth of school improvement literature advocating more collaborative, democratic and distributed forms of leadership, clear links with improved student outcomes have yet to be established.

A comprehensive review of the literature on headship and principalship has highlighted the paucity of evidence linking leadership at this level to improved student outcomes (Hallinger and Heck 1996a). Most recently in their systematic review, Bell *et al.* (2003) reinforce this general observation but suggest that 'distributed forms of leadership among the wider school staff is likely to have a more significant impact on the positive achievement off student/pupil outcomes than that which is largely or exclusively top down' (p. 3). For this reason, we need to understand much more about effective distributed leadership in action, how it can be nurtured, supported and developed. We need more empirical studies of distributed leadership that interrogate the relationship between distributed leadership and school improvement. But most importantly, we need to know whether distributed forms of leadership contribute to improved student outcomes and, if so, in what form?

Although some contemporary work has been completed and is reported later in this book, much more empirical evidence is required before any firm conclusions about distributed forms of teacher leadership and improved teaching and learning can be drawn. The evidence we currently have is incomplete and generally inconclusive about the precise nature of distributed leadership in action. For example, relatively little is known about how this type of leadership is maintained and sustained through different cycles of organizational development and change. In addition, the existing research base has not addressed the issue of contextual differences between schools and how this influences their ability to promote and implement distributed forms of leadership. More importantly, we are unclear about the impact of distributed leadership on schools, teachers or students. We urgently need contemporary, fine-grained studies of distributed leadership practice. While distributed leadership theory offers a dynamic and alternative way of understanding leadership practice, without the associated empirical base it is vulnerable and questionable. Conversely, there is a significant research base that has examined the relationship between teacher leadership and school improvement. This is explored in Chapter 3.

three

Teacher leadership and school improvement

Introduction

Successful school improvement is dependent upon the ability of individual schools to manage change and development. As Hopkins (2001) suggests, 'real' improvement 'is best regarded as a strategy for educational change that focuses on student achievement by modifying classroom practice and adapting the management arrangements within the school to support teaching and learning' (p. 2). As noted earlier, this necessitates building the 'capacity' for change and development within the school as an organization. Capacity building is concerned with creating the conditions, opportunities and experiences for development and mutual learning. Building the capacity for school improvement requires paying careful attention to how collaborative processes in schools are fostered and developed. In particular, it is concerned with maximizing teacher leadership and teacher learning. It suggests that where 'individuals feel confident in their own capacity, in the capacity of their colleagues and in the capacity of the school to promote professional development' (Mitchell and Sackney 2000: 78) school improvement is achieved.

Building capacity for school improvement implies a profound change in schools as organizations. Sackney *et al.* (1998: 52) argue that

> the post-modern era suggests a conception of organisations as processes and relationships rather than as structures and rules with conversation as the central medium for the creation of both individual meaning and organisational change. From this perspective, the image

> of schools as learning organisations seems like a promising response to the continuing demands for re-structuring.

This suggests a view of the school as a professional community where teachers have the opportunity to learn from each other and to work together. In such communities, leadership is distributed throughout the system and improvement 'occurs from an internal search for meaning, relevance and connection' (Mitchell and Sackney 2001: 139). Barth (2000) talks about 'creating a community of learners' where the prime purpose of the organization is to increase the capacity to bring about collective growth and development.

Capacity-building processes will obviously differ from school to school and from context to context. Of central importance in building learning capacity within organizations is the human perspective. By placing teachers at the centre of change and development, there is greater opportunity for organizational growth. Building the capacity for improvement means extending the potential and capabilities of teachers to lead and to work collaboratively. This can only be achieved as part of a democratic process where individual ideas and actions can be freely expressed. When a school operates democratically, teachers will be more likely to contribute to its development in a positive way (Harris 2002a).

The literature emphasizes that teacher leadership is not just concerned with teachers developing individually – a central role of teacher leaders is to help colleagues to try out new ideas and to encourage them to adopt leadership roles (Lieberman *et al.* 2000). Research has consistently underlined the contribution of strong collegial relationships to school improvement and change. Little (1990) suggests that collegial interaction at least lays the groundwork for developing shared ideas and for generating forms of leadership. Rosenholz (1989) argues even more forcibly for teacher collegiality and collaboration as means of generating positive change in schools. Collaboration is at the heart of teacher leadership because it is premised upon a redistribution of power within the school, moving from hierarchical control to peer control. In this leadership model, the power base is diffuse and the authority dispersed within the teaching community. An important dimension of this leadership approach is the emphasis upon collegial ways of working. For teacher leadership to be most effective, it has to encompass mutual trust and support. As West *et al.* (2000: 39) point out:

> If this leadership potential is to be realised, then it will have to be grounded in a commitment to learn and develop that inhabits the structures of schools as well as the classroom – it is likely that the school will conceive and act differently from the traditional explanations of leadership and structure.

Teacher leadership and school improvement

The literature on educational reform points unequivocally to the need for transformational approaches to leadership to secure organizational change and development (Fullan 2001). The work of Leithwood *et al.* (2004) suggests that the successful implementation of externally prescribed reform requires transformational leadership practice at all levels, but they are careful to point out that distributed and hierarchical forms of leadership are not incompatible. Their work demonstrates the need for distributed forms of leadership to be 'embedded within a complementary vertical leadership structure' that sets directions and provides resources (p. 76).

The school improvement literature similarly points towards high degrees of teacher involvement and collaboration as main levers for change. The literature suggests that distributing leadership to teachers, or 'teacher leadership', has positive effects on transforming schools as organizations and on helping to diminish teacher alienation (Rosenholz 1989; Little 1990; Hargreaves 1991). The school improvement research base has also highlighted that an organization's ability to develop largely depends upon its ability to foster and nurture professional learning communities, or 'communities of practice' (Holden 2002). Further evidence suggests that where teachers share good practice and learn together, the possibility of securing better quality teaching is increased (Lieberman *et al.* 2000). Such collaboration and collegiality are at the core of distributed leadership and have been shown to have positive effects upon teachers' self-efficacy and morale (MacBeath 1998).

Research by Crowther *et al.* (2000) reveals that teacher leadership is an important factor in improving the life chances of students in disadvantaged high schools. Silins and Mulford (2002) similarly conclude that student outcomes are more likely to improve where leadership sources are distributed throughout the school community and where teachers are empowered in areas of importance to them. Leithwood and Jantzi (2000) concluded that teacher leadership far outweighed principal leadership effects before taking into account the moderating effects of family educational culture. Evidence from this study suggests that principal leadership does not stand out as a critical part of the change process but that teacher leadership does have a significant effect on student engagement. The study concluded that distributing a larger proportion of current leadership activity to teachers would have 'a positive influence on teacher effectiveness and student engagement' (Leithwood and Jantzi 2000: 61).

Other research findings also suggest that empowering teachers to take on leadership roles enhances teachers' self-esteem and work satisfaction, which in turn leads to improved performance due to higher motivation, as well as possibly greater retention in the profession (Ovando 1996; Katzenmeyer and Moller 2001). In their study of 17 teacher leaders, Lieberman *et al.* (2000) reported that the teachers felt the experience had improved their confidence in their own abilities, and had taught them to motivate, lead and encourage other adults. Similarly, in their survey of 42 teacher leaders, O'Connor and Boles (1992) reported improved self-confidence, increased knowledge and an improved attitude to teaching.

Pellicer and Anderson (1995) found that, in the most effective schools, leadership was a shared responsibility of teachers and heads. Other studies also report positive effects of teacher participation in decision making, finding that teacher involvement in decision making leads to a reduction in teacher absenteeism (Sickler 1988; Rosenholz 1989). Two studies (Helm 1989; Leithwood and Jantzi, 1990) that describe how school leaders provide opportunities for teachers to participate in decision making and school development highlight the following:

- distributing the responsibility and power for leadership widely throughout the school;
- sharing decision-making power with staff;
- allowing staff to manage their own decision-making committees;
- taking staff opinion into account;
- ensuring effective group problem solving during meetings of staff;
- providing autonomy for teachers;
- altering working conditions so that staff have collaborative planning time;
- ensuring adequate involvement in decision making related to new initiatives in the school;
- creating opportunities for staff development.

In their longitudinal case studies of six schools, Weiss and Cambone (1994) found that while implementing reform proceeded more slowly where leadership was shared with teachers, it was generally accepted and implemented by all, whereas in schools with non-shared management, resistance continued. In his qualitative study, Griffin (1995) also found that the introduction of teacher leadership and the expansion of shared leadership encouraged the introduction of reform, and had positive school-level effects. In their study of school restructuring, Pechman and King (1993) found teacher leadership to be one of the factors affecting successful school reform. Similarly, Davidson and Taylor (1999) found that strong teacher leadership could mitigate the negative effects of frequent headteacher change in a restructuring school.

Benefits of teacher leadership

Under the right conditions, the positive benefits of teacher leadership are clearly identified within the literature. King (1996) and Griffin (1995) found that teacher leadership resulted in positive effects on pedagogy, school culture and educational quality. The research evidence also suggests that the success or otherwise of distributed leadership within a school can be influenced by a number of factors, including relationships with other teachers and school management. Empowering teachers in this way and providing them with opportunities to lead is based on the simple but profound idea that if schools are to become better at providing learning for students, then they must also become better at providing opportunities for teachers to innovate, develop and learn together.

The shared goals and values at the core of teacher leadership are also important in generating effective schools (Teddlie and Reynolds 2000). Ovando (1996) suggests that where teachers are placed in leadership positions, they are able to contribute more directly to organizational effectiveness and improvement. Some authors suggest that schools need to move from a hierarchical, top-down structure towards a more democratic model, in which teachers can directly influence development and change (Katzenmeyer and Moller 2001). A study of more than 600 teachers found that teacher participation in decision making was positively related to school effectiveness (Taylor and Bogotch 1994). Similarly, a longitudinal qualitative study of teachers who had taken on teacher leadership roles in restructuring schools found that teachers responded positively to their increased participation in decision making and that this directly contributed to school effectiveness.

In a study of British secondary schools, teachers generally felt that leadership was more effective where subject leaders and departmental heads were more strongly involved in decision making (Day *et al.* 2000). Pellicer and Anderson (1995) similarly found that in the most effective schools leadership was a shared responsibility of teachers and heads. Other studies have also reported positive effects of teacher participation in decision making. For example, Rosenholz (1989) and Sickler (1988) found that teacher involvement in decision making led to a decrease in teacher absenteeism and an increase in school effectiveness. Wong (1996) found that in schools with strong collaborative teacher–principal leadership, there was evidence of significant gains in pupil learning and achievement. Not all studies, however, have found such positive effects. For example, Peterson *et al.* (1987) found no relationship between shared decision making in schools and enhanced teacher effectiveness.

Effective schools place an emphasis upon the teaching and learning processes and invest in teacher development time. Of all the school-level characteristics, it is those that relate to teaching that have the most empirical support (Scheerens 1992). It is those factors that are most immediately proximal to, and therefore most immediately experienced by, students (i.e. teacher behaviours in the classroom) that will most immediately affect student achievement (Muijs and Reynolds 2001). As Smylie (1995) points out, teacher leadership can improve teacher effectiveness in a number of ways. The emphasis on continuous learning and excellence in teaching can improve the quality of teachers, while the emphasis on spreading good practice to colleagues can lead to an increase in the expertise of teachers throughout the school. The increased expertise and confidence of teachers, coupled with the greater responsibilities vested in them, will make teachers more willing to take risks and introduce innovative teaching methods, which should have a direct positive effect on teacher effectiveness.

Research by Katzenmeyer and Moller (2001) suggests that empowering teachers through teacher leadership improves their self-efficacy in relation to pupil learning. Teacher expectations directly relate to pupil achievement, hence strengthening self-efficacy is an important contributory factor of teacher leadership (Muijs and Reynolds 2001). Ovando (1996) found that when teachers took on leadership roles, it positively influenced their ability to innovate in the classroom and had a positive effect on student learning outcomes.

There is a body of evidence that demonstrates that teachers work most effectively when they are supported by other teachers and work collegially (Hargreaves 1994). Collegial relations and collective practice are at the core of building the capacity for school improvement (Hopkins 2001). It has been shown that the nature of communication between those working together on a daily basis offers the best indicator of organizational health. Hopkins *et al.* (1994) note that 'successful schools encourage co-ordination by creating collaborative environments which encourages involvement, professional development, mutual support and assistance in problem solving' (p. 177). It is therefore posited that teacher leadership necessitates moving away from traditional top-down management and getting teachers to take responsibility and to accept some accountability. Katzenmeyer and Moller (2001) assert that teacher leadership needs to be made available to all, otherwise some teachers will end up as leaders, while others are merely technicians, creating a two-tier system. The clear message from the literature is that school improvement is more likely to occur when leadership is distributed and when teachers have a vested interest in the development of the school (Gronn 2000; Jackson 2000).

Organizational barriers

The research evidence suggests that while teacher leadership is advantageous to the individual teacher and the school, there are several barriers that need to be overcome for genuine teacher leadership activity to occur in schools. One of the main barriers to teacher leadership identified in the literature is structural and concerns the 'top-down' leadership model that still dominates in many schools (Katzenmeyer and Moller 2001). Boles (1992) found that teachers' perceived lack of status within the school and the absence of formal authority hindered their ability to lead. Little (2002) found that the possibility of teacher leadership in any school is dependent upon whether the senior management team within the school relinquishes real power to teachers and the extent to which teachers accept the influence of colleagues who have been designated as leaders in a particular area.

Teacher leadership requires a more devolved approach to management and requires shared decision-making processes (Pellicer and Anderson 1995). Little (1995) found that for teacher leadership to be successful, some structural change was required within the school and that this did not necessarily mean relinquishing full control. Indeed, heads in the study claimed that, by introducing shared leadership, their influence on teaching in the school had increased. Magee (1999) identified support from the senior management team as a crucial component in the success of teacher leadership. The research found that where such support is not forthcoming, the possibilities of teacher leadership are dramatically reduced.

Ash and Persall (2000) argue that heads will need to become leaders of leaders, striving to develop a relationship of trust with staff, and encouraging leadership and autonomy throughout the school. For teacher leadership to develop, heads must also be willing to allow leadership from those who are not part of their 'inner circle' and who might not necessarily agree with them (Barth 1999). Weiss and Cambone (1994) found that in several schools heads started to impose more autocratic forms of leadership after about two years, following strong resistance from teachers to the reforms they were trying to implement. Wasley (1991) found that teachers need to be involved in the process of deciding on what roles, if any, they wish to take on, and must then feel supported by the school's administration in doing so.

Professional barriers

There are also professional barriers to teacher leadership that have been identified in various studies. Katzenmeyer and Moller (2001) suggest that teachers taking on leadership roles can sometimes be ostracized by their colleagues (Magee 1999). A number of studies have identified this as a significant barrier to teacher leadership. In their study of 17 teacher leaders, Lieberman *et al.* (2000) found that one of the main barriers to teacher leadership was often the feeling of being isolated from colleagues. Troen and Boles (1992) found that sometimes teachers felt less connected to peers when engaging in teacher leadership activities. Little (2002) found that while teachers were happy to acknowledge a hypothetical 'master teacher' or highly effective teacher, they were less inclined to accept their colleagues in leadership positions. However, in the school in which collaborative practices were well established, responses to teacher leaders proved to be more positive. The evidence shows that strong peer networks are a key source of support for teacher leadership (Zinn 1997). Little (2000) found a strong correlation between the degree of collaboration among staff and effective teacher leadership in action. Nemerowicz and Rosi (1997) and Harris (2001) suggest that teacher leadership will not occur unless it is underpinned by shared values. They argue that these shared values are developed first and foremost through shared (pedagogical) discussion, observation and team teaching. Hence, it is crucial that teacher leaders work in collaborative teams if they are to make a difference to the school.

In summary, research confirms that teacher leadership not only flourishes most in collaborative settings, but that teacher leaders should encourage the creation of collaborative cultures and develop common learning in schools (Griffin 1995; Caine and Caine 2000; Little 2000). Collective learning among staff and application of that learning to solutions that address students' needs is a central component of a professional learning community. Chapter 4 considers how schools can generate the capacity for development and the part teacher leadership plays in building professional learning communities.

Part 2

Enhancing teacher leadership

four

Building professional learning communities

Introduction

During the 1980s, the seminal study by Rosenholz (1989) found that teachers who felt supported in their own ongoing learning and classroom practice were more committed and effective than those who did not receive such confirmation. Teacher networks, cooperation among colleagues and expanded professional roles were all found to increase teachers' efficacy in meeting students' needs. Furthermore, Rosenholz (1989) found that teachers with a high sense of their own efficacy were more likely to adopt new classroom behaviours as well as to stay in the profession.

McLaughlin and Talbert (1993) confirmed Rosenholtz's findings by suggesting that when teachers have opportunities for collaborative inquiry and the learning related to it, they are able to develop and share a body of wisdom gleaned from their experience. Similarly, Darling-Hammond (1996) advocated that shared decision making was a core component of the transformation of teaching roles in some schools and for the building of a *professional learning community*. The idea of a school as a professional learning community defines itself: 'it is a school that engages the entire group of professionals in coming together for learning within a supportive and self-created community' (Morrissey 2000: 4).

Unfortunately, 'community' has come to mean any gathering of people in a school or social setting. But building a 'learning community' asks more of teachers than just simply gathering together. It assumes a focus on shared purpose, mutual regard, caring and integrity. It necessitates creating an environment in which pupils and teachers learn together. The development of such a community depends on three important and interrelated components: first, trust among those who are working together; secondly, knowledge of what the issues or tasks are that need to be addressed to move the school forwards; and, thirdly, the leadership capacity to undertake the necessary work in a way that allows modification and encourages reflection. At its most practical it provides a way of teachers working together to improve the learning experiences of young people.

The term 'professional learning community', therefore, is one that implies a commitment not only to teacher sharing but also to the generation of a school-wide culture that makes collaboration expected. Toole and Seashore-Louis (2002: 5) note that the term integrates three robust concepts: a school culture that emphasizes (1) professionalism – that is, is 'client orientated and knowledge based' (Darling-Hammond 1990); (2) learning – that is, places a high value on teacher professional development (Toole 2001); and (3) personal connection (Louis and Kruse 1995).

A professional community, therefore is, one in which teachers participate in decision making, have a shared sense of purpose, engage in collaborative work and accept joint responsibility for the outcomes of their work. Simply changing the organizational arrangements within schools will do little in isolation to promote pedagogical improvement. Concurrent attention must also be paid to building an infrastructure to support collaboration and create the internal conditions for mutual learning. This infrastructure provides a context within which teachers can improve their practice by developing and refining new instructional practices and methods.

A professional learning community

It has been suggested that 'developing a community of practice may be the single best most important way to improve a school' (Sergiovanni 2000: 139). In a learning community emphasis is placed upon the personal growth and development of individuals as a means of generating improved learning outcomes. In contrast, in a learning community there is a central commitment to building the capacity to learn – this is the end product, 'a living community that learns' (Mitchell and Sackney 2001). For schools, the implications are very clear. If schools are to sustain improvement over time, they will need to ensure that they are communities of learning. But how do schools become communities of learning? How do they generate the conditions in which learning can flourish and grow?

Currently, a major research project, 'Creating and Sustaining Effective Professional Learning Communities' (http://www.eplc.info/), is exploring the notion of a 'professional learning community' in the UK context. The project aims to examine:

- what a professional learning community is;
- what makes it effective; and
- how such a community is created and sustained.

Its broad aims are to provide:

- the characteristics of professional learning communities in different kinds of schools;
- key factors inside and outside schools that help or hinder the development of learning communities;
- innovative practices for ongoing professional learning and development.

The interim findings (McMahon *et al.* 2003) suggest that professional learning communities configure themselves differently according to context, phase, size and external plus internal conditions. The work also highlights the importance of trust and the quality of relationships as two important dimensions of building successful learning communities (Stoll *et al.* 2003). More work is underway but the initial results suggest that building professional learning communities is a complex and sometimes fraught process.

Little (2000) argues that there is no simple checklist or template that will ever adequately guide the formation of professional learning communities. She writes that 'there is a certain elegant simplicity to the problem of organising schools for teacher learning' (Little 2000: 233). To be most effective, professional learning communities need to exist within a social architecture that helps shape teachers' attitudes and practice. Toole (2001) suggests that this social architecture consists of the establishment of norms that govern behaviour (having a shared purpose), forms of ongoing interaction (reflective dialogue) and environmental conditions (social trust).

The main rationale for the development of professional learning communities in schools resides in the link between organizational change and pedagogical change. Until recently, little empirical evidence existed to connect the two, but an increasing number of studies now point towards the relationship between the establishment of professional learning communities and 'deep teacher change' (Toole and Seashore-Louis 2002: 12). Research has also highlighted that instruction is more effective in schools that are operating as professional learning communities (Rozenholz 1989) and that there are significant positive effects on student learning where the norms of collaboration and teacher learning are in place (Louis and Marks 1996).

The argument for building professional learning communities because of the impact on school and classroom improvement is compelling. As Hargreaves (2002) suggests 'professional learning communities lead to strong and measurable improvements in students' learning. Instead of bringing about "quick fixes" or superficial change, they create and support sustainable improvements that last over time because they build professional skill and the capacity to keep the school progressing' (p. 3). Yet there is some evidence to suggest that the evolution of professional learning communities is not 'always straightforward' or widespread (Toole and Seashore-Louis 2002: 5). Part of the problem may reside in the cultural variance across schools and, by association, their internal capacity to operate as a cohesive community, particularly in an external climate of competition, accountability and mistrust (Bottery 2002).

It would seem that without some external catalyst or source of agency to support the building of a social architecture of collaboration and mutual learning within schools, professional learning communities are unlikely to flourish. For example, the National College for School Leadership has been instrumental in introducing a major initiative aimed at building learning communities within and between schools. This is proving to be very successful and well received by schools. But whatever the origin or catalyst behind the building of professional learning communities in schools, the process of establishing ways of working among teachers that positively impact upon teaching and learning is of paramount importance. As Toole and Seashore-Louis (2002) point out, the 'ultimate goal is to link professional learning communities to improvements in teaching and learning' (p.3).

A recent study of especially effective schools by Newmann *et al.* (2000) concludes that building school capacity is the key to success and that forging professional relationships between teachers where they work and learn together is central to sustaining school effectiveness. Consequently, it is imperative that future efforts to improve secondary schools need to recognize the power and potential of departments to influence teachers, to generate change and to build professional learning communities. This is not simply to accept and endorse that such subject divisions are the best ways to organize the lives of students and teachers. It is to acknowledge that attempts at school improvement are more likely to succeed if development is undertaken at both the school and the departmental level and, by implication, where change efforts are located much closer to the classroom. This would suggest that all teachers have a role to play as leaders.

However, establishing a professional learning community requires dedicated and purposeful action on the part of the senior management team and the staff. The literature on professional learning communities repeatedly focuses on five attributes of such organizational arrangements: supportive and shared leadership, collective creativity, shared values and vision, supportive conditions, and shared personal practice. Each of these is discussed in detail by Morrissey (2000). A summary of the key features taken from her extensive literature review now follows.

Supportive and shared leadership

The school change and educational leadership literatures clearly recognize the importance of the headteacher and the senior management team in generating and securing school-level change. Transforming a school organization into a learning community is only possible with the sanction of the formal leaders and the active nurturing of the entire community. Louis and Kruse (1995) identify the supportive leadership of headteachers as one of the necessary human resources for restructuring staff into school-based professional communities. Sergiovanni (1994) states that 'the sources of authority for leadership are embedded in shared ideas' (p. 214), not in the power of position. Snyder *et al.* (1996) assert that it is also important that the headteacher believes that teachers have the capacity to respond to the needs of students, and that this belief 'provides moral strength for principals to meet difficult political and educational challenges along the way' (p. 19).

Collective creativity

In Peter Senge's (1990) book *The Fifth Discipline*, the idea of a learning organization is one 'where people continually expand their capacity to create the results they truly desire, where new and expansive patterns of thinking are nurtured, where collective aspiration is set free, and where people are continually learning how to learn together' (p. 3). As this idea was explored by educators and shared in educational journals, the term learning organization changed to 'learning communities'.

In schools, the learning community is demonstrated by people from multiple constituencies, at all levels, collaboratively and continually working together (Louis and Kruse 1995). Such collaborative work is grounded in what Louis and Kruse label 'reflective dialogue', in which staff conduct conversations about students and teaching and learning, identifying related issues and problems. Griffin refers to these activities as 'inquiry' and

> believes that as principals and teachers inquire together they create community. Inquiry helps them to overcome chasms caused by various specializations of grade level and subject matter. Inquiry forces debate among teachers about what is important. Inquiry promotes understanding and appreciation for the work of others ... And inquiry helps principals and teachers create the ties that bond them together as a special group and that bind them to a shared set of ideas. Inquiry, in other words, helps principals and teachers become a community of learners.
>
> (Griffin 1995: 154)

Shared values and vision

Sharing vision is not just agreeing with a good idea; it is a particular mental image of what is important to an individual and to an organization. A core characteristic of the vision is an undeviating focus on student learning, maintain Louis and Kruse (1995), in which each student's potential achievement is carefully considered. Such shared values and vision lead to binding norms of behaviour that the staff supports. In such a community, the individual staff member is responsible for his or her own actions, but the common good is placed on a par with personal ambition. The relationships between individuals are supported by open communication, made possible by a high amount of trust (Fawcett 1996).

Supportive conditions

One of the first characteristics cited by Louis and Kruse (1995) of individuals in a productive learning community is a willingness to accept feedback and to work towards improvement. In addition, the following qualities are needed: respect and trust among colleagues at the school and district level; possession of an appropriate cognitive and skill base that enables effective teaching and learning; supportive leadership from administrators and others in key roles; and relatively intensive socialization processes.

For learning communities to function productively, the physical or structural conditions and the human qualities and capacities of the people involved must be optimized (Boyd 1992; Louis and Kruse 1995). Louis and Kruse identify the following physical factors that support learning communities: time to meet and talk; small school size and physical proximity of the staff to one another; interdependent teaching roles; well-developed communication structures; school autonomy; and teacher empowerment.

Boyd (1992) presents a similar list of physical factors that result in an environment conducive to school change and improvement: the availability of resources; schedules and structures that reduce isolation; policies that encourage greater autonomy, foster collaboration, enhance effective communication, and provide for staff development. Time is clearly a resource: 'Time, or more properly lack of it, is one of the most difficult problems faced by schools and districts' (Watts and Castle 1993: 306). Time is a significant issue for faculties who wish to work together collegially, and it has been cited as both an obstacle (when it is not available) and a supportive factor (when it is available) as the case studies later in the book demonstrate.

Shared personal practice

In a professional learning community, a review of a teacher's instructional behaviour by colleagues is the norm (Louis and Kruse 1995). The process is based on the desire for individual and community improvement and is enabled by the mutual respect and trustworthiness of staff members. This practice is not evaluative but is part of the 'peers helping peers' process. Such reviews are conducted regularly by teachers, who visit each others' classrooms to observe, script notes and discuss their observations with the visited peer.

Mutual respect and understanding are the fundamental requirements for this kind of workplace culture. Teachers find help, support and trust as a result of developing warm relationships with each other. If one goal of reform is to provide appropriate learning environments for students, teachers also need 'an environment that values and supports hard work, the acceptance of challenging tasks, risk taking, and the promotion of growth' (Midgley and Wood 1993: 252). Sharing their personal practice contributes to creating such a setting.

In summary, the necessary features of a professional learning community are as follows (adapted from Morrissey 2000):

- The collegial and facilitative participation of the head, who shares leadership – and thus power and authority – through inviting staff input in decision making.
- A shared vision that is developed from staff's unswerving commitment to students' learning and that is consistently articulated and referenced for the staff's work.
- Collective learning among staff and application of that learning to solutions that address students' needs.
- Review of each teacher's classroom behaviour by peers as a feedback and assistance activity to support individual and community improvement.
- The physical conditions and human capacities that support such an operation.

Collectively, these features create the internal capacity for change, development and improvement. The next section explores the idea of capacity building in more depth.

Capacity building

The idea of 'building a school's capacity for development' is now widely known. Over the past 20 years, 'capacity building' has consistently appeared in the international reform literature. It was a very popular term in the 1970s and referred to creating the experiences and opportunities for people to learn how to do certain things. In the early 1970s, improving schools through capacity building meant that heads would organize the school for improvement, teachers would learn to work in teams, and teachers would talk publicly about what they were doing. The driving force here, although not stated explicitly, was the expansion or thickening of leadership. Without a clear focus on 'capacity', a school will be unable to sustain continuous improvement efforts or to manage change effectively. That we know. It is therefore critical to be able to explore, explain and illustrate the concept of 'capacity' in operational terms – this is more complex and elusive than it might at first appear.

From a relatively simple perspective, capacity building is concerned with providing opportunities for people to work together in a new way. Collegial relations are therefore at the core of capacity building. One of the distinguishing features of schools that are failing is the very absence of any professional community, discourse and trust. Within improving schools, a climate of collaboration exists and there is a collective commitment to work together. This climate is not simply given but is the deliberate result of discussion, development and dialogue among those working within the organization.

Capacity building is about ensuring that the school is a 'self-developing force' (Senge 1990) through investing in those school and classroom conditions that promote development and change (Hopkins and Harris 2000). The limitations of 'top-down' and 'bottom up' change are well documented. Both fail to recognize that unless the internal conditions within a school are predisposed to change and development, irrespective of how 'good' the new initiative or change is, it will inevitably flounder.

But what does capacity building look and feel like in practice? Hopkins and Jackson (2003) point us towards some useful central concepts and perspectives that offer an operational definition of capacity. The first is the central importance of the *people*, the leaders, educational professionals and students, and the expansion of their contributions. The second relates to the alignment and synergies created when internal arrangements, connections and *teams* are working optimally. The third corresponds to the organizational arrangements (the 'programme coherence' and the 'internal networks') that support *personal* and *interpersonal* capacity development. The fourth is more subtle, but crucially important. It is the territory of shared values, social cohesion, *trust*, well-being, moral purpose, involvement, care, valuing and being valued – which is the operational field of 'leadership'. The two key components of a capacity-building model are the professional learning community (the people, interpersonal and organizational arrangements working in developmental or learning synergy) and leadership capacity as the route to generating the social cohesion and trust to make this happen.

In this sense, capacity building is concerned with developing the conditions, skills and abilities to manage and facilitate productive school-level change. It also requires a particular form of leadership to generate school improvement, change and development. While the 'superhero' model of leadership may seem beguilingly attractive, evidence suggests that this approach to leadership is unlikely to generate the internal conditions for sustainable school self-renewal and growth. For this to be achieved, a new form of leadership is required, one that focuses upon learning (both organizational and individual) and one that invests in a community of learning – parents, teachers, pupils and governors.

Although there are no blueprints for successful school improvement, there are some core activities that have been shown to lead to cultural change. Some of the behaviours used to strengthen the school culture include reinforcing with teachers, norms of excellence for their own work, assisting teachers to clarify shared beliefs and values, and to act in accordance with such beliefs and values. These behaviours have been shown to encourage teacher collaboration, to increase teacher motivation and to improve teachers' self-efficacy. There is evidence to demonstrate a positive relationship between such approaches and school improvement. Culture building includes behaviours aimed at developing school norms, values, beliefs and assumptions that are pupil-centred and support continuing professional development. In summary, the goal of school improvement is to bring about positive cultural change by altering the processes that occur within the school. For long-term, sustained school improvement to occur, there has to be deep-rooted change inside the school.

Building capacity necessitates building an infrastructure of support that is aligned with the work of the school. This infrastructure involves the philosophy and mission of a school, the selection of personnel, resources (time, money and talent), teachers' training, work structures, policies and available outside networks. If a local education authority (LEA) supports the internal capacity building of a school, it would work with the school to develop and establish networks both locally and nationally.

Harris and Lambert (2003) argue that leadership capacity building can be defined as broad-based, skilful involvement in the work of leadership. This perspective involves two critical dimensions of involvement:

- *Broad-based involvement*: in the work of leadership by teachers, parents, pupils, community members, LEA personnel and universities.
- *Skilful involvement*: a comprehensive understanding and demonstrated proficiency by participants of leadership dispositions, knowledge and skills.

Throughout this book there has been an emphasis upon the centrality of the role of the teacher in the pursuit of school improvement. It has been emphasized that teacher leadership and teacher development are central to building the capacity for sustained school improvement. The evidence points to the importance of teachers working together and learning together in generating the capacity for change. However, while teacher collaboration may be highly desirable, it is not always easy to achieve in practice. In many ways, the design and organization of schools presents the biggest challenge to teacher collaboration and the building of learning communities. Teachers who do want to work together often find the barriers of time, competing tasks and physical geography difficult to overcome.

In summary, schools that improve and continue to improve, invest in the life of the school as a 'learning organization' where members are constantly striving to seek new ways of improving their practice (Senge 1990). An optimal school learning environment provides teachers with opportunities to work and learn together. It promotes the sharing of ideas and the open exchange of opinions and experiences. Teacher collaboration, reflection, enquiry and partnership are ways of building capacity for school improvement. This is something that teachers can and should actively create themselves. Constructing and participating in the building of professional communities in schools is, by its nature, a vibrant form of professional development. The next chapter will consider the relationship between professional development and school development.

five

Meaningful professional development

Introduction

Professional development is acknowledged across the world to be a central component in maintaining and enhancing the quality of teaching and learning in schools. The international research literature has consistently shown that professional development is an essential component of successful school-level change and development (Hargreaves 1994). It has confirmed that where teachers are able to reflect, access new ideas, experiment and share experiences within school cultures and with leaders who encourage appropriate levels of challenge and support, there is greater potential for school and classroom improvement.

Evidence also suggests that attention to teacher learning can impact directly upon improvements in student learning and achievement. Where teachers have clear professional identities and have intrinsic as well as extrinsic rewards for their work, they are more satisfied and committed and expand and develop their own teaching repertoires and, in relation to their purposes, it is more likely that they will provide an increased range of learning opportunities for students. In short, continuing professional development can have a positive impact on curriculum, pedagogy, teachers' sense of commitment and their relationships with students.

Continuing professional development is increasingly seen, then, as a key part of the career development of all professionals. The concept is often ill-defined, however, being in many cases conflated with the related concepts of in-service training and on-the-job learning. Both are more limited than professional development, as professional development can encompass a wide variety of approaches and teaching and learning styles in a variety of settings (inside or outside of the workplace). Professional development is also distinguishable from lifelong learning, which is a broader concept in that it can include all sorts of learning, whereas professional development is seen to be related to people's professional identities and roles and the goals of the organization in which they are working.

Much more is now known about the conditions under which teachers learn for the benefit of themselves and their pupils. The problem that remains is *how* to build learning communities within schools for teachers and pupils. These do not occur naturally. In many schools, the norms of practice are not those of collaboration or mutual sharing but tend to be isolation or 'balkanization'. While it is recognized that teachers' needs will vary according to circumstance, personal and professional histories and current dispositions, the matching of appropriate professional development provision to particular professional needs is essential if effective learning is to take place. This 'fit' between the developmental needs of the teacher and the selected activity is critically important in ensuring that there is a positive impact at the school and classroom level.

Where professional development opportunities are insensitive to the concerns of individual participants, and make little effort to relate learning experiences to workplace conditions, they make little impact upon teachers or their pupils. Building leadership capacity requires a constructivist approach to learning where teachers learn together and construct meaning from interaction, discussion and professional dialogue. Research has shown that to achieve improvements in teaching and better learning outcomes for students, teachers need to be engaged in meaningful professional development that promotes inquiry, creativity and innovation. Improvements in teaching are most likely to occur when there are opportunities for teachers to work together and to learn from each other.

Professional development

Schools that aim to build capacity and to generate professional learning communities will need to provide regular opportunities for teachers to engage in meaningful professional development. Professional development is continuous learning that it is the sum total of formal and informal learning pursued and experienced by the teacher, often under conditions of challenge. If the use of new practices is to be sustained and changes are to endure in schools, then teachers need to be able to engage in professional development that is collaborative and meaningful. Working collaboratively not only reduces the sense of isolation many teachers feel, but also enhances the quality of the work produced. Working as part of a professional development community helps focus attention on shared purpose and the goals that lead to school improvement and dynamic change.

There are several important messages about the role of professional development in building leadership capacity for school improvement:

- it is important to foster *deep collaboration* and not superficial cooperation among the teaching staff;
- it is important to form *partnerships* within schools and to network with other schools and agencies;
- It is important to generate *teacher leadership and pupil leadership*;
- it is important to provide opportunities for teacher *enquiry and action research*;
- it is important to allocate time for personal reflection and opportunities for teachers to talk together about *teaching and learning*;
- it is important to generate the *collective capability*, expertise and commitment of teachers to ensure that all teachers are involved.

Engaging regularly in continuing professional development is widely recognized as the tangible expression of the commitment to learn, and is essential if professionals at every level in the school are to remain up to date in their knowledge of the curriculum, be wise in their selection and use of a repertoire of pedagogical skills, be enthusiastic about their work and the students they teach, and be self-confident and clear about their purposes.

There are some schools where there is a culture of individualism and where processes of teaching and being a professional are rarely evaluated or discussed. It follows that teacher leaders themselves need to reflect upon their own practice. Yet despite the rhetoric of lifelong learning, research internationally continues to show that, for most teachers, formal development opportunities remain sporadic, occurring principally through short in-service education and training events. The extent to which other forms of development are available (e.g. critical friendships, mentoring, coaching, networking, action research) will depend as much on the leadership and learning culture of the school as upon the broader policy contexts or individuals' own inclinations or initiatives.

While the principle locus for learning remains the classroom itself, there can be some barriers to professional development. Research would suggest that these barriers are as follows:

- conditions of service for most teachers mean that little time is available;
- most teachers' learning is incidental, occurring in the classroom;
- teachers' learning lives are characterized by fragmentation and discontinuity;
- direct classroom experience seems to be the principal means for learning;
- few schools or individual teachers routinely plan for intervention by

others into their natural learning lives for the purpose of peer-assisted learning.

A key issue, then, in improving schools is how to provide opportunities for teachers to work together in an increasingly pressurized and changing profession. Although carried out almost 30 years ago, the seminal work of Argyris and Schön (1974) continues to provide a convincing explanation of the problems and possibilities for professional learning. They examined the work of people in several professions, including teaching, and characterized the 'normal' way of learning as 'single loop', in which 'we learn to maintain the field of constancy by designing actions that satisfy existing governing variables'. Promotion of this kind of learning is prevalent in school cultures that discourage systematic self and peer review of thinking, planning and practice. The problem with reflecting alone, however, is that there is a limit to what can be disclosed and what information can be collected and received by an individual with a 'vested' interest in avoiding uncomfortable change. Others are needed in the process.

Concepts of reflective practice, then, may be linked with those of collaboration. Peer partnerships and networks – discussions and dialogues between practitioners with common purposes – need to be encouraged to move from routine to reflective practice in schools. Many researchers have identified the dangers of parochial cultures that cut off schools from opportunities to open up and renew thinking and practice, and hence from any progress (Hargreaves 1994). Improving teaching, especially collectively, is more likely when practitioners articulate and examine the insights, values and strategies they bring to situations – in other words, when they engage in reflective practice.

Reflection and enquiry

The reflective teacher is one who turns attention to the immediate reality of classroom practice. Reflection is centrally concerned with improving practice rather than collecting knowledge. As each school, subject area and classroom are unique, reflective teachers develop their practice through engaging in enquiry and critical analysis of their teaching and the teaching of others. For teachers to be reflective about their practice, there has to be 'a feedback loop', a means by which they can consider their work in a critical way.

One powerful way in which teachers are encouraged to reflect upon and improve their practice is through a process of enquiry. Engaging teachers in the process of 'systematic enquiry' does not necessarily mean a detailed knowledge of research but rather involvement in a form of systematic reflection on practice. The argument for research as a basis for teaching rests upon two main principles. First, that teacher research is linked to the strengthening of teacher judgement and consequently to the self-directed improvement of practice. Secondly, that the most important focus for research is teaching and learning through the process of 'action enquiry'.

Action enquiry is essentially practical and applied. It is driven by the need for teachers to solve practical, real-world problems. The research is most usually undertaken as part of teachers' practice rather than a 'bolt-on' extra. Action research and enquiry is concerned with practical issues that arise naturally as part of professional activity. This practical orientation is one of the reasons why action enquiry remains a popular form of research activity among teachers. For teachers, values such as empowerment of learners and respect for students' views may be at the centre of their action enquiry activities. Improving practice is about realizing such values and necessarily involves a continuing process of reflection on the part of teachers. However, the kind of reflection encouraged by the action enquiry process is quite distinctive from an ends-driven type of reasoning. The reflection engaged in here is about choosing a course of action, or a particular set of circumstances, based upon a set of values or principles. Action enquiry improves practice by enabling teachers to make informed judgements about their own practice.

Collaboration

As noted earlier, improving schools engage teachers in a shared sense of purpose – a purpose made real by collaboration. Collaboration between teachers improves the quality of student learning essentially by improving the quality of teaching. It encourages risk taking, greater diversity in teaching methods and an improved sense of efficacy among teachers. Teachers are more able to implement new ideas within the context of supportive collaborative relationships or partnerships. By working collaboratively, teachers are able to consider the different ways in which the subject matter can be taught. Collaboration pools the collected knowledge, expertise and capacities of teachers within the subject area. It increases teachers' opportunities to learn from each other between classrooms, between subject areas and between schools. The insulated and often segregated departments of secondary schools make it difficult for teachers to learn from each other. Consequently, schools need to build a climate of collaboration premised upon communication, sharing and opportunities for teachers to work together. Collaboration is important because it creates a collective professional confidence that allows teachers to interact more confidently and assertively.

As highlighted earlier in the book, the skills needed for collaborative work include:

- developing a shared sense of purpose with colleagues;
- facilitating group processes;
- communicating well;
- understanding transition and change and their effects on each other;
- mediating conflict;
- developing positive relationships.

For collaboration to influence professional growth and development, it has to be premised upon mutual enquiry and sharing. There is sufficient evaluative evidence to show that when teachers are engaged in dialogue with each other about their practice, then meaningful reflection and teacher learning occurs. As teachers search for new understanding or knowledge with other teachers, the potential for school improvement is significantly increased. The school, as a learning community, is nurtured and sustained when individuals reflect upon, assess and discuss professional practice.

In summary, one of the most striking findings from the school improvement literature is that improving schools are marked by a constant interchange of professional dialogue at both a formal and informal level. It has been argued that creating a collaborative professional learning environment for teachers is the 'single most important factor' for successful school improvement and 'the first order of business' for those seeking to enhance the effectiveness of teaching and learning (Eastwood and Louis 1992: 215). Consequently, it is imperative that schools accurately assess professional learning needs and provide a wide range of meaningful professional development opportunities. The next chapter considers the types of professional development and support that can enhance teacher leadership.

six

Generating and supporting teacher leadership

Introduction

Throughout the previous chapters, attention has been paid to the ways in which a professional learning community can be generated. Encouraging teachers to be leaders similarly requires professional development, support and the opportunity to lead. Headteachers have been found to play a central role in generating and supporting teacher leadership. Buckner and McDowell (2000) found that to identify, develop and support teacher leaders in their schools, heads needed to encourage teachers to become leaders, to help teachers develop leadership skills, and to provide positive and limited constructive feedback. Similarly, research by Childs-Bowen *et al.* (2000) indicated that headteachers need to deliberately create the infrastructure to support teacher leadership and to offer opportunities to lead.

Building the infrastructure to support teacher leadership in schools, therefore, has a number of important dimensions. First, time needs to be set aside for professional development and collaborative work between teachers. Making time for planning together, building teacher networks and visiting classrooms is important. Ovando (1994) found that teachers reported decreased time for lesson planning and preparation once they had undertaken leadership roles and that this was considered to be detrimental. Seashore-Louis and Kruse (1996) similarly found that having time 'freed up' for teacher leadership tasks is a crucial element of success. Boles (1992) found that the factors for successful teacher leadership include principal support, strong communicative and administrative skills, an understanding of organizational culture and a re-examination of traditional patterns of power and authority in school systems.

Secondly, teacher leaders need opportunities for continuous professional development to develop their role. The research shows that to be most effective, teacher leaders need to continuously improve their teaching skills, be involved in school decision making and be involved in the professional development of others (Katzenmeyer and Moller 2001). Professional development for teacher leadership needs to focus not just on development of teachers' skills and knowledge, but also on aspects specific to their leadership role. Skills such as leading groups and workshops, collaborative work, mentoring, teaching adults and action research, need to be incorporated into professional development programmes to help teachers adapt to their new leadership roles (Katzenmeyer and Moller 2001). Furthermore, preparation for teacher leadership tasks can be impeded through lack of follow-up (Ovando 1996).

In the USA, formal training programmes for teacher leaders are widely available. These programmes include leadership skills such as rapport building, organizational diagnosis, dealing with change processes, finding and using resources, managing teacher workload, and building skills and confidence in other teachers. Hackney and Henderson (1999) advocate that heads and teachers should be educated together, breaking down the boundaries between the two forms of leadership to prepare all school staff for participation in truly democratic school structures. Sherrill (1999) has argued for the implementation of nationwide standards to provide clear guidelines for teacher leadership.

The success or otherwise of teacher leadership within a school is heavily influenced by interpersonal factors and relationships with other teachers and the school management team (Katzenmeyer and Moller 2001). The ability of teacher leaders to influence colleagues and to develop productive relations with school management, who may in some cases feel threatened by teachers taking on leadership roles, is therefore important (Lieberman 1988; Clemson-Ingram and Fessler 1997). Hostility to teacher leaders can arise through factors such as inertia, over-cautiousness and insecurity (Barth 1999). LeBlanc and Skelton (1997) reported that teacher leaders often experienced conflict between their leadership responsibilities and their need for affiliation and belonging to their peer group. Overcoming these difficulties will require a combination of strong interpersonal skills on the part of the teacher leader and changes to the school culture that encourage change and leadership from teachers.

Consequently, a third dimension of preparing teacher leaders is the need to equip them with good interpersonal skills. Lieberman *et al.* (2000) identified five main clusters of skills in their study of teacher leaders:

- building trust and rapport with colleagues;

- being able to undertake organizational diagnosis through data collection;
- understanding and managing change processes;
- being able to utilize resources (people, equipment) in the pursuit of common goals;
- building skills and confidence in others.

In addition, Pellicer and Anderson (1995) identified helping other teachers plan instruction, helping other teachers make curriculum decisions, helping other teachers improve their teaching and peer coaching as being the key skills of teacher leaders. Snell and Swanson (2000) found that teachers emerged as leaders if they developed high-level skills in the areas of expertise (strong pedagogical and subject knowledge), collaboration (working with other teachers, reflection on their own practice) and empowerment of themselves and others.

A final dimension of infrastructure support concerns teachers' motivation to undertake a leadership role. As Wagstaff and Reyes (1993) have pointed out, teacher leadership has the potential to increase the workload and, without adequate compensation, may lead to possible resentment. While research has shown that teachers do obtain intrinsic rewards through teacher leadership (increased effectiveness, increased influence, collegiality), these also come with strongly increased responsibilities. Hence, a consideration of some form of remuneration or reward for teacher leaders within the school is essential.

In summary, there are six dimensions of teacher leadership that require support and development:

- continuing to teach and to improve individual teaching proficiency and skill;
- organizing and leading peer review of teaching practices;
- providing curriculum development knowledge;
- participating in school-level decision making;
- leading in-service training and staff development activities;
- engaging other teachers in collaborative action planning, reflection and research.

By stepping out of the confines of the classroom, teacher leaders forge a new identity in the school and create ways of engaging others in development work. This new role embraces a belief that there are different ways to structure schools and a different way of working with teachers. In summary, the teacher leader is essentially a professional 'guide' who:

- models collegiality as a mode of work;
- enhances teachers' self-esteem;
- builds networks of human expertise and resource;

- creates support groups for school members;
- makes provisions for continuous learning;
- encourages others to take on leadership roles.

When teacher leadership is inextricably linked to teacher learning, it offers a powerful mode of professional development. The potential of this form of leadership to contribute to lasting school improvement is also more acute when teachers become more involved in professional decision making in school. Consequently, it is clear that developing and enhancing teacher leadership in this way has important implications for policy makers, practitioners and researchers. These will be explored next.

Implications for policy makers

There is evidence to suggest that teacher leadership has the potential to have a direct positive impact on school improvement and school effectiveness. There is also evidence to show that where teachers work collaboratively and where leadership responsibilities are devolved, teachers' expectations, morale and confidence are significantly enhanced. In addition, where teachers work collaboratively and share responsibilities, greater satisfaction is expressed among teachers for their work.

The implications for policy makers, therefore, concern issues of teacher professionalism, recruitment, retention and performance. While there are no immediate answers to the current problems facing the teaching profession in England, there are certain conditions that have served to exacerbate the present situation. For example, a lack of time for collaboration and shared teaching, a focus on attainment rather than learning, an emphasis on teacher as artisan rather than artist, and limited opportunities for research and reflection. In stark contrast, the teacher leadership literature highlights collaboration, learning, artistry and reflection as being at the core of teachers' professionalism and professional learning.

Implicit within teacher leadership is the notion of empowerment as teachers are given the responsibility and authority to act. Also inherent in teacher leadership is the establishment of professional community and an agreement about professional accountability. The evidence from the international community suggests that where teachers are prepared for and engaged in leadership activities, there are opportunities for professional development and growth that reinforce teachers' self-esteem and sense of self-efficacy. From a policy maker's perspective, teacher leadership offers one way of engaging the profession in forms of activities that are most likely to signal recognition, lead to reward and demonstrate trust in teachers to build their own professional learning communities within schools.

In short, teacher leadership offers policy makers a way of engaging teachers in a meaningful and timely debate about professionalism and issues of professional conduct. Essentially, the concept of teacher leadership endorses the principle that all teachers have the skills, abilities and aptitude to lead and should be trusted to do so. There is evidence from the literature of ways in which teacher leadership can be enhanced and developed. Furthermore, it reiterates how teacher leadership contributes to raising pupil performance, is pivotal in generating collaboration between teachers and in securing professional learning communities both within and between schools.

The next steps for policy makers would appear to be as follows. First, to investigate models of effective teacher leadership within the UK context and to identify exemplars of good practice. Secondly, to share and disseminate the principles and practice of good practice with schools and teachers. Thirdly, to evaluate the impact of introducing models of teacher leadership into different school contexts with a view to judging the effect upon teachers' professionalism and morale.

Implications for practitioners

The research evidence endorses teacher collaboration and mutual learning as centrally important to teacher leadership. It is clear that many schools are successful at promoting teacher collaboration and have set up ways of allowing teachers to work together. However, there are many schools where this has been more difficult to achieve because of structural or professional barriers. The implication of teacher leadership for schools, therefore, revolves around generating the possibilities and expectations of collaboration. Where this occurs, teachers are more likely to engage in high-level collaborative activities to improve their teaching capability and performance. In this sense, teaching becomes a highly reflective process that is reliant upon peer interaction, support and feedback.

The implications for schools of generating teacher leadership concern the provision of time plus support for research and enquiry. If teachers are to collaborate and reflect, they must be given time and support to achieve this most effectively. Similarly, structural barriers need to be removed to ensure that there are opportunities for teachers to work together outside their subject areas. Finally, if teachers are to be encouraged to take risks and to innovate, there has to be a real distribution of power and the agreement to uphold 'no blame' innovation.

Implications for research

Although the literature points towards the highly beneficial effects of teacher leadership upon schools and students, there is a relative absence of research that has explored the nature and impact of teacher leadership within the UK context. Research has focused upon teacher professionalism, collegiality, reflection and continuing professional development, but has taken little account of the models of leadership required to generate and sustain teacher learning and growth. Consequently, research is required that collects empirical evidence about teacher leadership in action, generates different models of teacher leadership, provides evidence of impact and effectiveness, illuminates good practice, and offers schools and teachers a clear insight into the possibilities and practicalities of promoting this form of leadership in schools.

The implications for research reside in the need for the collection of empirical evidence that:

- examines how far the concept of 'teacher leadership' is meaningful, useful and applicable to a wide variety of school contexts and circumstances;
- elucidates different models, approaches and forms of teacher leadership in practice;
- identifies how teacher leadership can best be facilitated and developed;
- investigates the relationship between teacher leadership and school improvement;
- provides case study exemplars of best practice and guidance for schools about creating the conditions in which teacher leadership can flourish and grow.

In summary, the concept of teacher leadership is powerful because it is premised upon the creation of the collegial norms in schools that have been shown to be effective and improving. It is also compelling because it is offers a way of building the internal capacity for change and development in schools. However, despite the claims made for teacher leadership and the evidence from the literature suggesting a strong relationship between teacher leadership and school improvement, there still remain relatively few contemporary studies that have explored this relationship in any depth. The next section explores some recent empirical evidence about teacher leadership and teacher effectiveness. It provides three case studies that show different degrees of teacher leadership in action.

Part 3

Recent studies and evidence

seven

Teacher leadership and teacher effectiveness

Introduction

It has been argued in previous chapters that developing leadership capacity is in itself a valuable goal. This is because of the clear benefits of teacher collaboration plus the associated improvement in teachers' self-efficacy and self-esteem. However, it is important to ask the harder question about whether teacher leadership contributes to enhanced teacher effectiveness and by implication improved student learning outcomes. This chapter considers these two related questions in detail and draws upon the school effectiveness research literature and recent findings from a contemporary study of teacher effectiveness to scrutinize the relationships between teacher leadership, teacher effectiveness and student learning outcomes.

The majority of school improvement and school effectiveness research reinforce findings that those factors closest to the classroom and the student are those that impact most positively on student learning. While it is recognized that there are powerful factors outside the control of the school, such as socio-economic factors, prior attainment and social class, which are all powerful predictors of subsequent educational attainment and achievement, school-level factors also have a significant influence on student learning outcomes. These factors relate directly to what goes on in the school as an organization and the most important of these is individual teacher effectiveness. The school effectiveness research base has consistently highlighted significant 'within-school' variation at the teacher and the subject level. It is clear that teachers' effectiveness can vary quite considerably even within the same department, subject area and with the same group of children. This has led researchers to support what is known as 'proximity theory', that factors affect student learning in order of their proximity to student experience (Muijs and Reynolds 2002).

But what exactly do we mean when we talk about teacher effectiveness? The first issue to consider is how effectiveness is defined. This has been a matter of some debate and controversy within the educational community, but effectiveness is measured essentially in terms of students' academic performance using either value-added or raw score measures. However, pupils' well-being, self-confidence, self-esteem and social skills are clearly also important outcomes of the teaching and learning process. But the difficulty of measuring these outcomes with any precision has meant that 'effectiveness' has generally been measured largely but not exclusively in the currency of academic outcomes.

The second issue about teacher effectiveness is what teachers need to do to achieve these outcomes. The research evidence shows that several things appear to make a difference. One of the most important is the nature or type of teachers' classroom behaviour – that is, what teachers actually *do* in the classroom. How do they manage their classroom? How do they interact with students? What classroom climate do they create? These behavioural factors have been widely identified as being important determinants of teachers' subsequent effectiveness (Mortimore *et al.* 1988; Muijs and Reynolds 2000, 2002, 2003) using student learning outcomes measures identified by standardized test scores. From the point of view of proximity theory, it is what teachers do in the classroom that most directly affects student learning outcomes; therefore, it is not surprising that teachers' behaviours are such important influences on subsequent learning.

Research has shown that teachers' beliefs about their subject and how best to teach it are also powerful influences on student learning and achievement (Harris 1999). The notion of 'pedagogical content knowledge' draws attention to the importance of teachers' knowledge about their subject area, especially the instructional strategies and pedagogical practices that will optimize student learning. These implicit beliefs about teaching the subject have a strong influence on teachers' classroom practice and teaching behaviours. Two recent studies that focused upon connectionist beliefs (the belief that teaching is based upon dialogue between teacher and students, which helps teachers to better understand their students and allows students to gain access to teachers' knowledge) found that this shaped teachers' classroom behaviour and guided their classroom practice.

Similarly, teachers' belief in their self-efficacy – that is, the extent to which they feel they are effective teachers (Askew *et al.* 1998; Muijs and Reynolds 2003) – has been shown to influence subsequent teaching practices and pedagogical approaches. In one recent study of teachers' effectiveness (Muijs and Reynolds 2003), it was shown that teachers with higher self-efficacy tend to be more effective compared with teachers who possess low self-efficacy. In this sense, teachers' inherent beliefs about themselves, their subject and their students are powerful influences upon their classroom behaviour and have been shown to be very difficult to change. Similarly, personal factors such as teachers' own need for achievement and affiliation have been found to affect their classroom behaviour and, by association, to indirectly affect student outcomes.

Teacher leadership and teacher effectiveness: what does research tell us?

As teacher effectiveness is such an important factor in determining student achievement and attainment, the central question must be whether and to what extent teacher leadership positively affects teacher effectiveness? We know that the nature and quality of leadership within schools is important for maximizing school effectiveness and improvement. Many studies have reached the same conclusion about the importance of leadership in securing improved performance at school and student level. However, as noted earlier in the book, this form of leadership tends to be automatically equated with the leadership of the headteacher or principal and not necessarily with leadership at other levels within the school organization. At best, the leadership of the principal or headteacher will have an indirect effect on performance at the school or teacher level. Inevitably, this form of leadership is mediated through the actions of teachers and administrators within the school. Recent evidence points towards the closer and direct relationship between teacher leadership and pupil learning outcomes (Silins and Mulford 2002).

The emphasis on research and collaborative activity associated with teacher leadership could be important here. If teachers become active researchers and reflect upon their practice, it is likely that they will change both their beliefs and behaviours. Similarly, by engaging in collaborative activity with other teachers and leading innovation and change, it is possible that implicit beliefs may be challenged and practices altered. In this way, teacher leadership is a catalyst for changing beliefs and behaviours and is thus directly associated with effectiveness. Engaging in teacher leadership is also associated with increases in teachers' self-esteem and self-efficacy. Once again, it is likely that such positive personal developments are likely to impact positively upon teachers' classroom effectiveness.

The relationship between teacher leadership and teacher effectiveness is implied rather than proven. Studies of this relationship are not readily available, though the evidence available points towards the likelihood of there being a positive relationship between the two. Interestingly, the research evidence shows that high achieving schools tend to be more confident in allowing teachers to take on leadership roles. As one North American study showed, improving student outcomes was a condition for rather than a result of teacher leadership (Dickerson, 1992). Once again, the relationship here is suggested rather than proven.

Most research on teacher effectiveness has tended to concentrate on identifying particular generic skills, abilities or traits that render one teacher more effective than another (Brophy and Good 1988). There has been a desire to identify those features, factors or characteristics of effective teachers so as to nurture, enhance and promote teachers' effectiveness. Inevitably, this has generated several lists of characteristics of effective teaching but has not shed light on exactly *how* teachers become effective in different contexts, cultures and school settings. Furthermore, the research base has also highlighted that effectiveness is not a uniform measure but that variation in teacher performance is the norm. In other words, within any school there is likely to be some differential between levels of teachers' effectiveness.

The five-element model proposed by Campbell *et al.* (2003) offers one way of understanding differential teacher effectiveness and its wider significance for understanding school effectiveness. This model proposes that teachers may be differentially effective in five separate domains. It is suggested that teachers can be differentially effective in how successful they are in teaching pupils of different backgrounds (i.e. different abilities, prior knowledge, gender and social background), with different learning styles and dominant intelligences, and can be differentially effective in different contexts (schools) and roles (such as relations with parents and indeed leadership roles). Teacher leadership, with its emphasis on continuous reflection and action research, has the potential to contribute to enhancing the quality of teaching in these five domains. Leithwood and Jantzi's (2000) study, which showed a modest, indirect effect of teacher leadership on student learning outcomes in a large-scale survey of Canadian teachers, is an important indicator of the potential of teacher leadership to influence effectiveness. Similarly, a study of 86 US middle schools found that both teacher professionalism and collegial leadership were positively related to student outcomes (Hoy *et al.* 1998). Another study has also suggested that encouraging teachers to take on leadership roles positively affects self-efficacy and behaviour (Lemlech and Hertzog 1998). The authors reported that those teachers who exhibited more collaboration, sharing of good practice and participation in committees and decision making showed greater self-efficacy. Both sharing good practice and higher self-efficacy have been explicitly linked to effective teacher behaviours in a number of studies (e.g. Muijs and Reynolds 2003).

The San Francisco Math Leadership Project attempted to improve teacher effectiveness and teacher leadership skills simultaneously. As part of this project, over 500 teachers attended a year long programme addressing teacher effectiveness and confidence in maths, as well as teacher leadership skills that should allow teachers to share their expertise with colleagues throughout the system. Teachers in the programme instigated a number of leadership activities within their schools and there is some evidence to suggest that their teaching effectiveness was improved. This highlights another aspect of the relationship between teacher leadership and teacher effectiveness, which is the opportunity that teacher leadership provides for effective teachers to have a positive influence on the pedagogy of other teachers in their school, thus contributing to overall improvement in the effectiveness of teaching. There is evidence to suggest that if teachers are empowered and their disciplinary knowledge is valued, experimentation and new modes of teaching are more likely to develop and teaching effectiveness is likely to increase (Vasquez-Levy and Timmerman, 2000).

Some researchers appear to view teacher effectiveness almost as a constituent of teacher leadership (e.g. Krisko, 2001). Although, as we have seen, this is not entirely without empirical confirmation, no contemporary studies have explored the relationship between teacher leadership and teacher effectiveness in any depth. The following section examines the findings from a study conducted in England that offered an opportunity to explore this relationship and to explore the relative benefits to teachers and schools of teacher leadership.

The Gatsby Teacher Effectiveness Study

The relationship between teacher leadership and teacher effectiveness is explored here using the data from a much broader empirical base that comprised the Gatsby Teacher Effectiveness Study (Muijs and Reynolds 2000). This large-scale project was conceived and designed to explore the dimensions, contours and components of effective teaching in primary and elementary mathematics. The research programme was part of the evaluation of the Primary Mathematics Enhancement Programme, funded by the Gatsby Charitable Trust.

A large amount of data was collected as part of the Gatsby Project. To examine the relationship between teacher leadership and teacher effectiveness, we focus on the data from the fourth year of the project. This data set involved 23 primary (elementary) schools in two local education authorities (districts) that were involved in the Gatsby Project. Three control or comparison schools in another local education authority were also included in these analyses. All teachers in years 1, 3 and 5 in one authority, and years 2, 4 and 6 in another authority were observed twice a year (autumn and summer term) during maths lessons by trained observers, giving a total of over 240 observations. The inter-observer reliability had earlier been established as 81%. More than 2500 pupils were involved. An observation schedule developed for the project, the Mathematics Enhancement Classroom Observation Record (Schaffer *et al.* 1998), which was based on a number of existing reliable instruments such as the Special Schools Observation System, was used in the classroom. During lessons, the observers made detailed notes of classroom interactions and behaviours. After each lesson, the occurrence and quality of 65 different types of teacher behaviours were rated on a scale of 1–5.

All pupils were tested using standardized numeracy tests, which were administered twice a year, once in March and again in July. These tests were designed to accord with the English National Curriculum in mathematics. The scores on the tests had a reliability (Cronbach's alpha) of > .8 in all years in this study (see Table 7.1). Data on free school meal eligibility, English comprehension, special needs status and gender were also collected from the school and formed part of the broader analysis.

Table 7.1 Who is involved in decision making in the school?*

	School A (high teacher leadership)	*School B (developing teacher leadership)*	*School C (failing teacher leadership)*
SMT only	0%	11%	37%
SMT and MM	14%	77%	37%
SMT, MM and teachers	86%	12%	26%

* Percentage of responses coded in each category. SMT = senior management team, MM = middle managers.

In the fourth year of the project, a range of school-level data was collected by researchers interviewing maths coordinators and senior managers. The interview schedule was based on research on school effectiveness, and included a range of questions related to this. Questions addressing teachers' involvement in decision making and the administration of the school were also posed. Following the interviews, the data were coded and each school was given a score on a range of variables. Scoring was done by a researcher who was not involved in the classroom observations or the analysis of the quantitative data, and who therefore did not have any *a priori* knowledge of the scores for teacher behaviours or pupil outcomes.

Previous studies had shown that it was possible to assess teachers' effectiveness in teaching mathematics. The evidence showed that effective teachers tended to score highly on a range of variables across areas and that these scores were consistently high (Muijs and Reynolds 2001, 2002, 2003). The research also showed that teacher effectiveness was related to pupil outcomes. Teachers who scored higher in the effectiveness range correlated positively with pupils scoring highly in tests. While prior achievement was found to be the most significant predictor of subsequent performance, as demonstrated in many previous studies, we found that teacher effectiveness was a stronger predictor of pupil attainment than free school meal eligibility, special needs status, gender or ethnicity.

To illustrate the point, if two pupils had the same score on the beginning-of-year tests, the same free school meal eligibility, gender, age, ethnicity and special needs status, the pupil taught by the most effective teacher would score up to 20% higher on the end-of-year test than the pupil taught by the least effective teacher. Consequently, the relative effectiveness of the teacher makes a significant difference to pupil attainment and achievement. But what influences effectiveness? Is there any evidence to suggest that teacher leadership makes any difference to a teacher's effectiveness or not? A secondary analysis of the data focused upon the relationship between teacher leadership and core dimensions of teacher effectiveness. The first relationship we explored was whether teacher leadership, as disaggregated to levels of involvement in decision making, is related to teacher effectiveness in terms of the positive behaviours observed.

Teacher leadership and teacher effectiveness

To explore the relationship between teacher leadership and teacher effectiveness, a correlation analysis was undertaken (see Table 7.2). As teacher leadership is a complex construct, it was important to take one element or feature that would adequately represent teacher leadership in any statistical analysis. The literature on teacher leadership consistently identifies involvement in decision making as a key indicator of the strength of teacher leadership (Muijs and Harris 2003). Consequently, involvement in decision

Table 7.2 Do teachers ever initiate decisions in the school?*

	School A (high teacher leadership)	*School B (developing teacher leadership)*	*School C (failing teacher leadership)*
Teachers often initiate decisions	100%	25%	20%
Teachers are consulted	0%	75%	80%
Teachers are not consulted	0%	0%	0%

* Percentage of responses coded in each category.

making was used as a proxy measure for teacher leadership within the statistical analyses undertaken.

Before looking at the results of the analyses, it is worth reiterating how correlation analyses needs to be understood. Correlations measure the relationship between two variables. The correlation coefficient varies between –1 (perfect negative relationship, e.g. if teachers are more involved in decision making, they are less effective teachers) and +1 (perfect positive relationship, e.g. if teachers are more involved in decision making, they are more effective teachers). A correlation of 0 reflects no relationship at all. A correlation coefficient > .5 is seen as a strong relationship; a correlation > .3 is seen as a moderate relationship; a correlation > .1 is seen as a modest relationship; and a correlation < .1 is seen as a weak relationship.

From Table 7.1 we can clearly see that teacher involvement in decision making has a moderate to strong relationship with almost all teacher behaviours we measured. Relations are strong with correcting behaviour, asking open questions and elaborating on answers, explaining key points, encouraging student interaction and communication, and creating a welcoming and pleasant classroom.

Another measure of teacher effectiveness is whether pupils are on task during lessons. This was measured during classroom observations by the researcher counting which pupils were visibly on or off task every 5 minutes. This variable is also related to teacher involvement in decision making: where teachers are more involved, pupils are more likely to be on task during lessons (correlation of .25).

A technique called 'multi-level modelling' was used to ascertain whether teacher involvement in decision making could explain some of the variance in teacher effectiveness (measured as a composite of all the individual variables in Table 7.1), taking into account the percentage of students eligible for free school meals, percentage of students with special needs, average school achievement level, percentage of boys and percentage of pupils from ethnic minorities. A number of school effectiveness variables were also added, including teacher motivation, leadership factors and school context. Teacher effectiveness was therefore predicted by all these factors, and by teacher involvement in decision making.

We found that when we included teacher involvement in decision making, in comparison to the other variables the unexplained variance decreased by 14%. It was a highly statistically significant predictor of teacher effectiveness, which would suggest that teachers' involvement in decision making and, by association, teacher leadership contributes to their effectiveness in a very positive way.

Teacher leadership and pupil outcomes

Teacher involvement in decision making and pupil achievement was the next relationship explored. First, teacher involvement with pupil outcomes was correlated directly. This revealed a weak but significant relationship between teacher involvement in decision making and pupil gains over the year (correlation of .07). It is not surprising that the direct relationship is weak if we consider the elements of the proximity model highlighted earlier. However, the analysis undertaken attempted to reveal whether and to what extent teacher involvement in decision making had a stronger indirect relationship on teacher behaviours and subsequent pupil attainment: This was tested using a method called structural equation modelling (see Fig. 7.1).

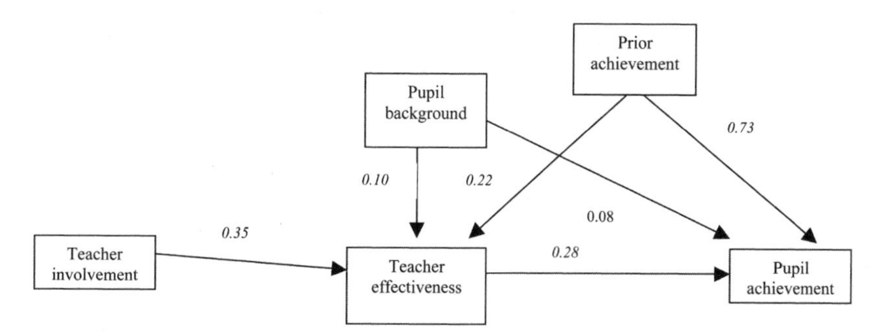

Figure 7.1 Results of structural equation modelling.

This model examined whether teacher leadership had an indirect effect on pupil achievement through its influence on teacher behaviour, having first controlled for the effect of pupil background factors (i.e. free school meals, special needs, ethnicity and prior achievement). The values shown in Fig. 7.1 are the standardized coefficients. Like correlation coefficients, these vary from −1 to +1. In summary, teacher involvement in decision making was the factor most strongly related to teacher effectiveness, more so than pupil background and prior achievement, and the relationship was positive. Teacher effectiveness was, in turn, related to achievement at the end of the year, although unsurprisingly the effect of prior achievement was stronger. The indirect effect of teacher leadership on student outcomes was also calculated, which was found to be significant. Overall, the total (direct and indirect) effect of teacher involvement was stronger than that of student background, although weaker than that of prior achievement.

Although these findings suggest a positive relationship between teacher leadership and teacher effectiveness and, by association, positive gains in student attainment, it is important to offer an alternative interpretation of the results at this point. It could be that the direction of causality is not, as we hypothesized here, from teacher leadership to teacher effectiveness, but from teacher effectiveness to teacher leadership. It is possible that headteachers or principals who have more confidence in certain teachers and their effectiveness are more likely to give them more responsibility and to involve them in decision making. Similarly, more effective teachers may be more self-confident, and therefore more likely to take on leadership roles. Nevertheless, the results are promising in that they point most strongly to the positive elements of this relationship.

The Gatsby Teacher Effectiveness Project demonstrated that teacher involvement in decision making offered a good proxy for teacher leadership and showed, that as a proxy, it was always moderately or strongly related to teacher effectiveness. The analysis also demonstrated that there was an indirect relationship between teacher involvement in decision making, teacher effectiveness and higher student outcomes. Although this research base is inevitably limited, it does allow some modelling to explore how teacher leadership affects teacher behaviours and, ultimately, student achievement.

In summary, this analysis and the findings from other studies highlighted in this chapter suggest that there are several reasons to believe teacher leadership is positively related to teacher effectiveness. It is clear that the degree of involvement in decision making is important for teachers' self-efficacy and self-esteem. There is also evidence to suggest that improved self-efficacy and self-esteem impact positively upon teachers' effectiveness and, ultimately, secure higher levels of student attainment and achievement. While it would be unwise to overclaim the potency of teacher leadership, it is clear that it can contribute to teacher effectiveness and is a positive part of teachers' professional growth. The next chapter explores the relationship between teacher leadership and differential effectiveness in more depth.

eight

Teacher leadership and differential effectiveness

Introduction

As highlighted in the previous chapter, teacher effectiveness research has been conceptualized as being located primarily in the relationship between teacher behaviours and subsequent student learning outcomes (see, for example, Brophy and Good 1988; Muijs and Reynolds 2002). In other words, a teacher is effective if student test scores rise or there are other indications of improvements in academic outcomes and performance. Much research has explored the characteristics of effective teachers and effective teaching in an attempt to inform practitioners and policy makers about the optimum way of designing and teaching the curriculum. Certain countries have taken this a stage further by developing appraisal mechanisms that specifically focus on teacher classroom performance or, in some cases (such as Tennessee), their pupils' performance on state tests. In this sense, teacher effectiveness can become both a mechanism of accountability and a tool for evaluating a teacher's classroom skills.

Using teacher effectiveness for accountability purposes has a number of related issues or problems that are worth highlighting. First, operating with a generic model of teacher effectiveness means that it is impossible to factor in specific variables, such as school type, school context, school culture plus the particular features of the subject, class and curriculum content. Taking a broad view of teacher effectiveness delimits the possibilities of refining the model to apply it to different school or classroom settings. Secondly, researchers, particularly in the UK (e.g. Harris 1999; Muijs and Reynolds 2001), have drawn increased attention to the need for a more differentiated model of effectiveness that takes into account a wider range of variables and factors. Work has been undertaken at the level of the secondary school department (e.g. Sammons *et al.* 1997; Harris 2000c) that demonstrates quite clearly that there is wide variation of performance at this level. The research shows that teacher effectiveness is intrinsically related to the overall effectiveness of the department. It not only contributes to this effectiveness but is also a product of the way in which the department is managed, organized and led.

Thirdly, it is increasingly recognized that the existing models of teacher effectiveness focus on one part of a teacher's work only – that is, instruction – whereas teachers' time is taken up with many other tasks that could be used to make judgements about their effectiveness. Recent empirical studies of teachers' work (e.g. Campbell and Neill 1994) show that teachers typically spend only about one-third of their extended working time on classroom instruction (including planning and marking), with a range of extra-classroom activities, such as meetings, curriculum development, social and welfare tasks with pupils and parents, school management and leadership roles, and professional development, taking up the remainder. Under the auspices of various reform initiatives, the volume of work outside classrooms has increased, especially the administrative load on teachers (e.g. Campbell and Neill 1994; Tedesco 1997; Day *et al.* 2000; Klette 2000).

The resulting attention to the 're-modelling' of the workforce agenda in England is the latest acknowledgement of the expanding demands and duties placed on individual teachers. By implication, this means looking for a definition of effectiveness that includes how effectively the teacher manages other adults in the classroom, including teaching assistants, technicians and other para-professionals, as well as managing pupil behaviour and pastoral matters. It is clear that the single measure of cognitive gain by students cannot stand as proxy for all these activities or indeed be a robust measure of teacher effectiveness in the current climate. In light of these changes, an appraisal of teacher effectiveness concentrating exclusively on the teacher's ability to instruct classes directly would appear to be inappropriately narrow.

As noted in Chapter 7, Campbell *et al.* (2003) have suggested that at least five different areas of differentiated effectiveness can be identified. These are now discussed in some detail. First, there is the issue of differential effectiveness across different subjects in the curriculum, or across different components. Evidence from Ofsted inspections of primary schools is beginning to demonstrate that the same teacher can be judged to be outstanding in, for example, mathematics but only adequate in teaching history or physical education. This is because the inspections now provide a profile of teacher performance in relation to each lesson observed (typically up to four lessons in an inspection). The lessons are commonly of different subjects.

Although there is as yet limited evidence about different performance in different subject components (algebra as against number in mathematics, for example), because the inspection data are not presented at that level of detail, there is no logical reason not to believe that a teacher can perform differently in different subject components. This analysis is not restricted to primary schools; secondary teachers teach subjects other than their specialism, especially to younger pupils, and the argument about subject components applies equally to them as to their primary colleagues. Thus a differential model would need to include a consistency dimension across the instructional role.

Secondly, teachers may be differentially effective in promoting the cognitive progress of different groups of pupils according to background variables. The principal ones are ability, age, sex, socio-economic status and ethnicity. For example, a teacher might be extremely effective in promoting the learning of pupils with special educational needs but less so with very able pupils, or vice versa. Any model of differential effectiveness would need to be able to identify such strengths and enable the interactions among these variables to be examined.

Thirdly, teachers may be differentially effective in promoting the learning of pupils according to the pupils' personal characteristics, such as their personality, cognitive learning style, level of motivation and self-esteem. Fourthly, teachers may be differentially effective in response to the various contexts in which they work. For example, effectiveness may be different in a two-teacher rural primary than in a 2000-pupil urban comprehensive school; in different departments or faculties in the same school; in homogeneous, than in heterogeneous classroom groups; in schools with strongly framed cultures than in schools with weakly framed cultures. This would require a model in which the interrelationships between school context and teacher effectiveness are reflected. At the present time, recognition of this issue is reflected in the adoption of the term 'educational effectiveness', but its use may serve to blur matters by avoiding the need to tease out the interactions, which in many contexts are extremely complex.

Finally, teachers may be differentially effective in the various different roles they perform. These include the important pastoral and welfare roles teachers are increasingly asked to perform, developing relationships with parents and the community and, finally, the leadership roles they can take on in their schools. The next section explores the skills required to take on leadership roles in schools.

Teacher leadership in action

There is an increasing focus on teachers' differential effectiveness and in particular its contribution to school effectiveness. There is a growing expectation that teachers need to be effective across all five of the domains highlighted earlier; however, the question has to be asked whether it is reasonable or realistic to expect teachers to have all the skills and to be effective in all these roles. It is also important to ask about the relationship between these five areas and teacher leadership. While the empirical base is relatively thin, there is some evidence to suggest that the skills required of teachers as active leaders are different from those routinely expected. Looking at teacher leadership from a differentiated perspective, there are a wide range of skills and abilities that can be identified. These have been categorized by Harris and Lambert (2003) (see Table 8.1).

Table 8.1 Teacher leadership skills

Personal actions	**Collaborative skills**
Listening to feedback	Decision making
Self-reflection	Team building
Self-evaluation	Problem solving
Concern and respect	Resolution of conflicts
Professional skills and knowledge	**Change agency**
Responsiveness	Planning
Communication	Change
Influence	Professional development and support
Professional knowledge	

It is clear from the list in Table 8.1 that a great deal is asked of teachers as leaders and it is acknowledged that not *all* these skills will be highly developed in all teachers. Consequently, collaborative ways of working and teamwork can bring individuals with different skills together and can help alleviate the demands of teacher leadership roles. This mutual sharing has been termed 'community knowledge' or, in other words, a 'social movement' within the school or organization (Wenger *et al.* 2002). The basic idea is that the participation of people at different levels of readiness, including those new to the profession plus support staff, build momentum over time and that leadership action is emergent rather than immediate. The advantage of this participative, emergent approach is that it opens up a wide range of development options and enables individuals to learn from each other in a meaningful and mutually supportive way.

Building a 'knowledge system', as Wenger *et al.* (2002) describes it, among teachers is a complex undertaking. It is clear that communities of teachers working together will go through their own phases of development and change as they attempt to influence organizational change and development. Wenger *et al.* (2002: 196) have identified five life-cycle phases of a knowledge system or community of practice: prepare, launch, expand, consolidate and transform. These are very similar to the stages of development identified in the team-building literature (i.e. forming, norming and performing) or in the change literature (i.e. initiating, implementing and continuation).

In phase 1, teachers who are working together prepare the way by agreeing exactly what they need to focus on or change. Recent work by Little (2000) has shown that the initial dialogue among teachers about what needs to be achieved and how far there is a consensus on this is a particularly critical part of the preparation phase. In addition, the important issue of communication systems and processes needs to be resolved to enable the group to move on. In phase 2, the ideas or areas for development will be shared with other teachers or 'launched' in the sense that they now belong to the organization rather than the group. In phase 3, the work of the group expands by involving other teachers and/or spreading to other subject or curriculum areas. The process gains momentum through various combinations of top-down directives and encouragement and bottom-up initiatives and responsiveness.

In phase 4, the work of the group becomes consolidated in that the process of implementation has been successful and the development work is becoming part of the fabric of the organization, in so far that it is becoming institutionalized. In phase 5, the group itself transforms into something new or different. Wenger *et al.* (2002: 205) suggest that the transformation potential is twofold. First, communities become more than an integral way of bringing about change as they become the focal structure. Secondly, communities do not merely transform how the school operates but they transform it continually. This suggests that the school has so deeply incorporated the values associated with mutual learning that transformation is part of the culture. The transformational potential of communities in organizations hinges on the 'paradox of cultivating informal structures as opposed to managing them in conventional ways' (Wenger *et al.* 2002: 217). Communities of teacher leaders are informal and non-permanent groupings that provide new opportunities for innovative thinking. They are essentially the central agents of change.

However, these informal groupings do not gel together automatically. There have to be incentives, support mechanisms and rewards for teachers who choose to lead in this way. As mentioned earlier, two factors that can hinder the adoption and success of teacher leadership in schools is lack of teacher time and the perceived lack of reward for teachers who take on these often demanding leadership roles (Harris and Muijs 2003). If leadership is explicitly acknowledged as being part of the role of teachers in policy and practice, it is more likely that time and resources will be freed to allow teachers to exercise leadership roles.

Little (1995) explored the question of organizational legitimacy for teacher leaders in her work which documented the evolution of leadership in two secondary schools in the process of restructuring. She identified two central issues – 'contested ground' and 'leadership legitimacy' – and found that teacher leaders found themselves caught between strategies of commitment versus control. When teachers work on new developments or lead innovation, there is an inherent tension between collaboration and the bureaucratic structures that support teaching and learning, such as timetabling and the need for curriculum coverage. Little (1995) suggests that this is 'contested ground', as there are opposing forces that operate in the school and on the teachers. To be effective, teacher leaders need to learn to negotiate between these two forces and move their school forward despite the inherent pull towards the *status quo*.

In summary, this chapter has looked at the relationship between teacher leadership and differential teacher effectiveness in more detail. It has explored the range of skills required to be an effective teacher leader and considered the phases of working effectively as a learning community. We argue that if teacher leadership is to be prevalent in schools, it will require a re-conceptualization and re-definition of what it means to be a teacher and how teaching performance is assessed or evaluated. The next chapter considers some of the benefits of and barriers to teacher leadership in action. Through the lens of a recent research project funded by the General Teaching Council and the National Union of Teachers, a contemporary insight into teacher leadership is provided. The findings from this project are summarized and the conditions that support teacher leadership in schools are outlined.

nine

Teacher-led school improvement: a research study

Introduction

Although the literature points to the highly beneficial effects of teacher leadership upon schools and students, relatively little research has explored the nature and impact of teacher leadership within the English education context. A great deal of research has focused upon the leadership of the headteacher, but little account has been taken of alternative conceptualizations or models of leadership, particularly those that address issues of teacher learning and growth. In 2003 the General Teaching Council for England (GTC), in conjunction with the National Union of Teachers (NUT), commissioned a research project to explore the extent to which teacher leadership, as a distinctive form of professional collaboration for school improvement, had some legitimacy and cogency in schools in England. Within the project, 'teacher leadership' was defined as: 'the capacity for teachers to exercise leadership for teaching and learning *within and beyond the classroom*'.

Initially, an extensive literature review funded by the GTC was undertaken (Muijs and Harris 2003) to explore the empirical and theoretical base underlying the concept of 'teacher leadership'. This work provided the conceptual and analytical framework for a research project involving ten schools where teacher leadership had been identified. This research project built upon the initial literature review by exploring teacher leadership in practice and providing contemporary evidence of teacher leadership in action. In particular, the project's aims were to:

- identify different models of, and approaches to, teacher leadership in practice;
- explore how teacher leadership can best be facilitated and developed;
- explore the possible relationship between teacher leadership, as a form of professional collaborative work, and school improvement.

The operational definition of teacher leadership used in the research was one derived from the literature and premised upon purposeful collaboration and cooperation among teachers. It is not leadership as defined by formal role or responsibility (e.g. an assistant head or a subject coordinator), but as collective agency and professional collaborative action with a pedagogical purpose.

A case study design was adopted for the project. Qualitative evidence was collected from ten school case studies covering a variety of contexts and circumstances. These schools were initially identified by local education authority (LEA) advisers, national bodies and external projects on the basis that there was evidence of teacher leadership in the school that was considered to be contributing to improvement. Care was then taken to select ten case study schools that encompassed a range of variables (sector, geographical location, gender, ethnic mix) and reflected a mixture of external initiatives (e.g. networked learning communities, education action zones, external school improvement initiatives).

It is acknowledged that in a small-scale study of this type, generalizations to a national picture are difficult to make. However, the study does provide some contemporary cameos of teacher leadership in action and offers some insights into this form of professional collaborative action in practice. In summary, the case study analysis allowed: an exploration of teachers' understandings of the concept of teacher leadership; contemporary insights into teacher leadership and forms of teacher collaboration in action; an analysis of the benefits of teacher leadership to classroom and school improvement; an exploration of the conditions that enhance and support teacher leadership.

Understanding teacher leadership

The research found that 'teacher leadership' was not a term generally used by those in schools. For most teachers in the study, the idea of leadership was not a word they readily associated with their own activities, even though many of them were leading initiatives and developments. However, the project found that 'teacher leadership' could be a meaningful concept to teachers when it was introduced as a way of describing professional collaboration or engagement for a specific purpose – for example, developing new curriculum materials, planning joint teaching or preparing for peer observation. Teachers tended to use 'collaboration, partnership and networking' to describe ways of working with other teachers and the term 'teacher leadership' was considered to be one way of describing these collective activities. In short, the research found that teacher leadership is connected with professional initiative and learning, both within and between schools, that is focused on improvement at classroom, department/ year group and whole-school levels. For example, one teacher reflected:

> I would say it's either leading a department, a year team, or making improvements, I imagine. It doesn't necessarily mean you're a head of department, or head of year, it could be having responsibilities in that you have got to make improvements.

In many cases, it appears the questioning about 'teacher leadership' triggered thought about the issue and an acknowledgement that teachers took leadership roles within the school even though this was not generally known as 'teacher leadership'. For the majority of respondents in the study, teacher leadership was widely viewed as positive, and as being a key contributing factor to school improvement, by harnessing teacher creativity and energy. The head of one secondary school, that had seen many improvements over the last five years, commented:

> The improvements in the school are hugely down to teachers taking responsibility for leadership. We [the senior management team] can't do it all ourselves. We can provide the vision, but at the end of the day, we've got to rely on people implementing the Numeracy strategy, the Literacy strategy, and so on.

Another member of a senior management team said:

> If you disempower teachers, you actually end up creating a blame culture, where people just look round for other people to poke when things go wrong. So what I wanted to do was set up a culture that empowered people.

The evidence points towards a deliberate attempt by those in formal leadership roles to create the conditions in which teachers feel involved in decision making and in shaping the future development of the school:

> Last year there was very much an atmosphere of shared leadership – natural and organic, happening when it needed to. (advanced skills teacher)

> What we're trying to do is break down the hierarchy. (advanced skills teacher)

The research found that there were five dimensions of 'teacher leadership,' as a form of professional initiative and learning. The first was *shared decision making*, whereby teachers were given responsibility to make decisions on behalf of the school on important developmental work. The second was a form of *collaboration*, in which they operated collegially for the prime purpose of securing certain outcomes linked to improving teaching and learning. The third was *active participation*, whereby teachers understood teacher leadership in terms of being actively involved in core developmental tasks and being a participant in the process of school improvement. The fourth was *professional learning*, in which teachers learned individually and with colleagues. The fifth was *activism*, whereby teachers engaged with issues on behalf of the school in an effort to directly affect change and development. Using these five dimensions, teacher leadership can be viewed as an organizational quality generated through particular forms of teacher interaction and partnership.

Shared decision making and involvement

There was recognition among the headteachers of the schools of a need to give teachers more responsibility for change and development as a way of building human capacity within the organization. How far this translated into action was an issue probed by the study. The data showed that shared decision making rarely meant that classroom teachers were fully involved in making decisions. When teachers were involved in the decision-making process, this usually took the form of individual or collective consultation with the senior management team. In most cases, schools actively supporting teacher leadership extended decision-making opportunities to those in formal leadership positions (i.e. to middle management). Consequently, while the possibility of shared decision making existed in all of the schools visited, in practice teachers were not always fully involved in the process. As one teacher noted:

> Since the new management has come in ... as a staff we have become increasingly more involved with everything that's happened. We've much more influence over what has happened. We have meetings where we have input into things.

In all the schools visited, teachers were strongly encouraged to lead on initiatives, and were supported by senior management in doing so. A wide range of initiatives taken by teachers was reported during the interviews. In one school, a newly appointed teacher started a drama course at GCSE level within the school. In another school, a young PE teacher led on the sports college bid the school was making. A maths head of department had led on introducing the Key Stage 3 strategy and was now recognized as a leading maths teacher in the LEA, training teachers in other schools. In one school, an administrator had successfully led a drive on improving attendance, which was described as highly successful. In one school, according to the deputy head:

> A teacher in her first year organized the sports day and a rock-climbing event. That is a big initiative for someone in their first year. We didn't say 'ah, you're too young, you can't do this'. We said 'yeah, ok, but with the right support and guidance'.

What is striking from the study is the degree of autonomy given to teachers, some young and inexperienced, to lead on important issues for the school. Within all the schools there was a general view that all teachers had the potential to lead and that this was not only the preserve of more experienced members of staff.

> We felt that our experiences were really valued by others in the school, even though we've only been teaching since September. It does feel as though we are making a difference within our own departments. (newly qualified teacher)

However, it was acknowledged that changing from more established styles of leadership was not easy. As one head from a successful rural school, commented, 'I have tried to become more consultative over time, but sometimes it's difficult to change your habits'.

The research also found that varying amounts of involvement extended to support staff and that this contributed to a collective sense of being involved in decision making:

> Our learning assistants are linked to a faculty. From the leadership aspect they're involved. They attend faculty meetings and have a say in what happens and they give us feedback, which is really useful, as they're always with us and can see each class developing. It helps us develop our practice as well. (newly qualified teacher)

The data suggest that even in schools that support forms of teacher leadership, the traditional expectations of the head as leader can prove to be a major barrier to establishing alternative ways of working and distributing leadership responsibilities throughout the organization.

What does teacher leadership look like in schools?

Using the five dimensions identified above, the research found a wide variety of formal and informal groupings characterized as 'teacher leadership'. It is clear that the changing educational climate towards federations, partnerships and networks has afforded more opportunities for teachers to collaborate and has provided a renewed legitimacy for teacher collaboration. Four of the schools were involved in external initiatives or programmes aimed at promoting collaboration. Two were involved in 'Networked Learning Communities' (NLC), one in 'Improving the Quality of Education for All' (IQEA) and one in 'Best Practice Networks' (Specialist Schools Trust). These initiatives had prompted new groupings among teachers both within and across schools. These groupings were predominantly subject-based or were action research groups with a mandate to undertake developments or to problem solve in certain key areas for the school or schools.

In the other case study schools, teacher collaboration and networking was not externally driven or configured. It consisted of informal groupings between teachers for particular purposes. In one primary school, for example, teams of four or five teachers were working to secure improvement in English and the arts. This group met regularly to discuss curriculum, teaching and learning issues, and to plan developmental work. As a result, the team produced new materials for Key Stages 1 and 2, which were shared with staff and which formed the basis of in-service training with other schools. Other examples include an initiative by the head of modern foreign languages to introduce a new set of methods to improve pupils' communication skills in foreign languages and a maths teacher who had worked with colleagues to rewrite all the maths schemes in the department to fit in with the National Numeracy Strategy.

There was some evidence that where teacher collaboration was facilitated by externally funded projects (i.e. NLCs, IQEA), there were more opportunities for teachers to meet with each other both within and across schools. The four schools involved with these initiatives agreed that this external support had enhanced teachers' professional initiative and innovation significantly, particularly through the provision of additional resource and time. In contrast, those schools without external support found it more difficult to provide teachers with time to meet and inevitably felt that their collaborative efforts were constrained because of this.

Creating the culture

There were several factors that appeared to enhance leadership capacity and helped teacher leadership to emerge in schools. One major factor concerned school culture, in particular the extent to which there was a sense of collegiality and a shared vision among staff:

> They are all fully aware of the way forward, they are consulted on the school's strategic vision, they know they are responsible in this area,

so I know I can let them get on with it and their particular team can meet the school vision. (secondary head)

The data suggest that teacher leadership can only be fostered and nurtured in a culture that is supportive and where relationships among staff are positive. A high degree of trust is required for teachers to lead initiatives, instead of the senior management team, and therefore in schools where the culture is not collegial the possibility of teacher leadership is inevitably reduced.

We're a very small tight-knit team and we're all very experienced teachers, so we were able to operate with less structure and procedure because everybody was willing to cope with things happening on an *ad hoc* basis. (advanced skills teacher)

Favourable cultural conditions for teacher leadership were created through certain structural arrangements. In the schools in the study, there were opportunities to switch roles and responsibilities. As one head noted: 'There are lots of opportunities for staff to move around in school [post wise]'.

Regular meetings with the whole school staff, monitoring meetings with line managers and opportunities to meet together to jointly plan new initiatives were key components in building leadership capacity in the schools. Some teachers suggested that explicit opportunities for reflection should be built into the school day. All teachers in the study had the opportunity to regularly discuss teaching and learning issues with colleagues. They also contributed to staff meetings, although some younger teachers felt that contributions were not always appreciated or welcome, even in schools that strongly encouraged teacher leadership. As one young teacher commented: 'Most of the time you can contribute. But I think sometimes you do feel uncomfortable 'cos you know people will disagree with what you're saying'.

Encouraging internal promotions and providing opportunities for continuing professional development were seen to contribute to a positive school culture that supported teacher leadership alongside the support of senior management. What is clear is that the cultural conditions need to be optimum for teacher leadership to flourish, but that giving teachers some leadership responsibility is one way of generating the internal conditions for change.

Barriers to teacher leadership

The study found a variety of barriers to the development of teacher leadership. Three main categories emerged from the data, the first of which was the external educational context. External accountability mechanisms, especially in poorly performing schools, placed a heavy burden of accountability on teachers and on senior management that made the distribution of leadership more difficult and more risky.

The proliferation of top-down initiatives emanating from central government was similarly viewed as stifling teacher initiative and leadership capabilities. The inherent tension between the pressures of accountability and the demands for development within schools clearly affected how teachers viewed their role.

The second barrier to teacher leadership relates to this particular tension, as teachers' capacity to undertake 'extra work' was seen as a limiting factor. The lack of time for teachers to engage in activities outside of classroom teaching and administration was a key inhibitor to teacher leadership: 'One of the big inhibitors is time. They are willing and they are able, but they have to have a life at the end of the day'.

Some teachers also felt that they were lacking in experience and confidence when taking on leadership roles. Also, according to some senior management team members, teacher leadership was inhibited by general teacher apathy and a lack of willingness to take on new responsibilities.

Finally, the role of senior managers in some cases was seen as a barrier, especially where the senior management team was unwilling to relinquish control, where leadership from the head was seen as weak, or where senior managers were poor communicators. In addition, a lack of clarity about teachers' roles and responsibilities can make teacher leadership problematic. As one teacher commented, 'I think if roles were more clearly defined it would be easier. You sometimes get the impression that you can do something, and then someone says "oh no, you shouldn't have done that"'.

The benefits of teacher leadership

The research found that activities associated with 'teacher leadership' – for example, teacher collaboration, partnership or professional networking – had a positive effect on teachers' morale and sense of self-efficacy. The evidence highlighted that where teachers were engaged in collaborative forms of activity, they expressed a high degree of ownership and involvement in the development work of the school. Parenthetically, this was considered to engender positive feelings of professional self-worth and to improve motivation. As one teacher summarized:

> In the past, we were solving problems alone, working independently. By working together, we solve problems together and we support each other. Working this way is not only productive but an excellent way of

> feeling valued by others and good about your own capabilities. (teacher, case study school A)

The data also suggested that teachers were more likely to stay in schools where a culture of teacher collaboration and leadership existed. The benefits of working with other teachers and being able to take on individual initiatives and leadership roles was identified by three or four teachers in the study as a major reason to stay at the school. One teacher, for example, commented that:

> There are no barriers to teacher initiative here. I would have felt that in other schools. I think that's one of the reasons I stayed here. Because as a supply teacher I went to many schools and this was one of the toughest [in terms of pupil intake]. (teacher, school 6)

The research found that shared leadership can be a positive lever on teacher retention and recruitment. For example, in two of the schools, the new members of staff interviewed had chosen the school primarily because of prior knowledge about existing opportunities for collaboration and networking with other teachers and schools.

Research has shown that where teachers are given significant responsibility for school development and change, their work can have an impact on school improvement. There was evidence within this study of developmental work undertaken by teachers impacting directly on the school and contributing to improvement. For example, a group of teachers in a secondary school had taken responsibility for developing materials and resources to support the use of accelerated learning techniques in different subject areas in Key Stage 3. These materials were made available across the school and further work is being undertaken at Key Stage 4. Departmental evidence and data would suggest that these materials were making a positive contribution to the quality of teaching and to learning outcomes.

Enhancing teacher leadership

The evidence demonstrated positive outcomes associated with the activities and outcomes from different forms of teacher leadership. However, it also found that ten conditions need to be in place to ensure that the potential of teacher leadership is maximized. These conditions are as follows: (1) a supportive culture; (2) strong leadership (i.e. support from the headteacher, senior management team and governors); (3) commitment to action enquiry and reflection; (4) innovative forms of professional development; (5) coordinated improvement efforts; (6) high levels of teacher participation and involvement; (7) data richness; (8) collective creativity; (9) shared professional practice; and (10) recognition and reward.

Supportive culture

Within each of the case study schools, there was evidence of a culture that supported teacher leadership, collaboration and partnership. Teachers were actively encouraged to lead initiatives within the school and it was clear that there was a 'no-blame' stance taken to innovation work that was less successful. There were processes in place for sharing ideas such as regular staff meetings, newsletters, away-days and INSET days, plus the mechanisms created by external initiatives. In most of the schools, there was also evidence of pupil engagement in research activities and in some aspects of developmental work through providing feedback or through collecting different forms of data (photographic, written, taped). Another important element of the school's culture was a high degree of trust. As one subject leader said:

> I think trust in this school is very strong, and we've worked hard as a school to develop that. We had a day closure where we talked about building learning communities. We went right back to grass roots and said how do we see learning, and how do we want the school to be managed and led to promote learning? (teacher, school 7)

Strong leadership

At each of the case study schools, there was strong support and direction from the headteacher and the leadership team for teachers working together. This support was seen as instrumental in ensuring that all staff were aware of the importance of the work and cooperated with each other. There was a shared view that without the support from the headteacher and other members of the leadership team, these activities were unlikely to flourish. The research literature on teacher leadership concludes that the headteacher's support is central to the success of shared or distributed leadership. These research findings reinforce this view and also point to the need for the support of governors, particularly when developments have school-wide implications.

> It would be difficult to undertake this type of work without the support of the head or the senior team, as so much depends on being able to take other staff with you. Our governors are also supportive of our work as they know it is making a difference. (teacher, school 3)

Commitment to action enquiry and action research

Within each school there was a great deal of commitment to various forms of action enquiry and action research. The majority of working groups were engaged in data collection of some form for the prime purpose of informing development. Three of the schools had dedicated their INSET days to consider action enquiry methods and four schools were receiving expert input on data collection and enquiry from external initiatives. It was felt that the training had contributed significantly to the work of the group and the subsequent quality of the developmental activities.

Innovative forms of professional development

There was evidence within most of the schools in the study of innovative approaches to professional development. While all schools engaged in INSET days, these were often led by staff within the school or by staff from other schools. An emphasis was placed on knowledge transfer through the various groupings within and across schools. There was also evidence of peer tutoring and mentoring across themes and subject groupings. Essentially, the models of professional development that were prevalent across the case study schools were premised on collective rather than individual learning.

In one primary school, a coaching and mentoring programme was put in place to help develop leadership skills in the members of the newly constituted senior management team. This programme was subsequently expanded to all staff. Within the school, middle-level leaders work as mentors for new staff and help them develop their subject leadership roles. In summary, there is a high degree of involvement in leadership development from within the school and this is considered to be a way of building the school's leadership capability.

Coordinated improvement efforts

In all cases, teachers and senior staff recognized the need to coordinate the various areas of activity or developmental work within the school. This was achieved by regular meetings between the working groups and the senior management team. In these meetings, updates on progress were provided and any resource issues discussed. In addition, the senior management team in each school carefully monitored the work of the groups and considered engaging in external initiatives only if this complemented their work. For example, one school became involved in Networked Learning Communities because it reinforced what they were already doing and complemented the leadership approaches that the school was endorsing.

High levels of teacher participation and involvement

It was noticeable at each school that the development work was not confined to a small group of teachers. The headteachers made every effort to ensure there was broad participation and representation in working groups and in the various initiatives. It was clear that teachers had a temporary membership of working groups or networks with the understanding that other members of staff could step in and take over their activities. This way staff perceived any new initiative or development as involving them even though they might not be involved initially or directly. As one secondary teacher put it: 'There is an emphasis on shifting roles and responsibilities; that way leadership is constantly changing and evolving'. The research found that a high level of engagement and involvement of staff in the developmental work of the school promoted high self-esteem and a willingness among teachers to engage with new ideas.

Data richness

Each of the case study schools was actively involved in collecting a wide variety of data. In certain cases, pupils were also engaged in data collection and feedback to staff. Data were collected with the prime purpose of informing subsequent development. In one school, a group of teachers collected data about teacher assessment at Key Stage 1. This subsequently was turned into a best practice guide for teachers at the school. Also, in three of the schools there was a particular emphasis upon pupil data and engaging pupils as researchers. Within these schools, pupils were involved in collecting data that would contribute to the work of the school improvement groups or those teachers involved in the networked learning community.

Collective creativity

An emphasis on collaboration and mutual sharing at the schools meant that teachers were encouraged to share ideas and to problem solve together. The study found that teachers felt that this way of working together was most likely to generate a collective creativity that was both innovative and rewarding. The innovative work in the case study schools had resulted from the work of groups rather than individuals and there was a consensus that it was possible to produce more innovative and creative work by working collaboratively:

> By working with the other members of the NLC [networked learning community], we have been able to generate ideas that would have been

> more difficult to reach as an individual school or as a small group of teachers from one area. (teacher, school 8)

Shared professional practice

One of the main benefits of collaborative ways of working is knowledge generation and knowledge transfer. Within the study, there was evidence that teachers were sharing knowledge but also sharing professional understanding and practice. For example, in one networked learning community, teachers from the same subject had taught in other schools for the prime purpose of demonstrating certain classroom techniques or pedagogic approaches. This exposure of professional practice was shown to have a powerful impact on other teachers and contributed significantly to their professional learning.

> One of the major benefits of working together is the possibility of seeing other types of teaching and learning new techniques and approaches from teachers with different styles or approaches. (teacher, school 2)

Recognition and reward

Within each of the case study schools, there was a great deal of support for professional recognition of the work undertaken. An emphasis was placed on dissemination both within schools and between schools. Where possible and appropriate, teachers were rewarded but it was clear that most of the professional activities were not formally recognized through external accreditation opportunities. Teachers in the study felt that some form of external recognition or accreditation for their efforts would be very helpful.

In summary, the study found evidence of teachers leading change in schools to varying degrees. It was clear that some schools in the study were further forward than others in creating the conditions where teacher leadership could flourish and grow. Crowther *et al.* (2000) suggest that 'teacher leadership produces positive school outcomes' and there is some evidence to show that teachers were having a positive influence on their school through their development work. However, the extent to which they could have a positive influence was dependent on a number of factors that will be explored in depth in the next three chapters. These chapters provide detailed case studies of teacher leadership in action. They are intended to be both illuminative and illustrative of the ways in which teacher leadership is manifesting itself in contemporary school contexts. They also highlight the differences between schools in cultivating and nurturing teacher leadership.

ten

Successful teacher leadership

Introduction

As noted earlier in this book, there are few contemporary studies of 'teachers as leaders' in schools in England. As a consequence, the operational images of what teacher leadership looks like are not readily available and how teacher leadership is developed and sustained in schools is based upon limited empirical evidence. The GTC/NUT study allowed detailed data to be collected on a number of schools where teacher leadership was in evidence. This and the next two chapters provide case studies from this GTC/NUT study with the prime purpose of illuminating the different ways in which teacher leadership manifests itself in schools. The three cases show high, medium and low levels of teacher leadership, respectively. The intention is not to offer any judgement about the schools or the teachers, but simply to illustrate how differing degrees of teacher leadership can affect the potential for school development change and improvement.

School A

The first case study is that of a large primary school serving a socio-economically disadvantaged estate in the suburbs of a medium-sized coastal city in England. The estate, from which the school draws all its pupils, consists largely of council-owned rented housing. Some private housing exists, largely properties bought by former council tenants under the 'Right to Buy' legislation. There is a great deal of poverty on the estate, and many single-parent families. There are two other primary schools serving the same catchment area. The school has performed below the national average in terms of test results over several years.

All staff at the school were asked to provide their views on the extent to which they felt that there was evidence of teacher leadership at their school. The data collected allowed teachers to offer their confidential views on a number of issues related to teacher leadership. For the purpose of the data collection, teacher leadership was operationalized as: decision making, initiating decision making and amount of involvement. The data revealed that there was a general consensus among staff in the school that decision making was largely a shared process. Table 7.1 shows responses to this item for all three schools (see p. 76). It is clear that most staff in school A felt that decision making was shared not just between the head and middle managers, but between head, middle managers and teachers. In contrast, in schools B and C, the majority of teachers felt decision making largely resided with the senior management team and middle managers.

The interview data collected at school A reinforced the view that decision making is seen as emanating either from the head or from teachers or middle managers, depending on specific circumstances and decisions. As one classroom teacher put it: 'Any decision would either come from Sally downwards or from us upwards through the senior management really. It would depend, but we can take initiatives as teachers'. Similarly, all the staff in school A felt that teacher initiative was strongly supported in the school. Again by contrast with schools B and C, teachers in school A unanimously felt that they could initiate decision making.

The qualitative evidence revealed that there is a high degree of support for teacher initiative within school A. For example, as one teacher noted, 'I go to courses or meetings with the LEA, and I just sort of take initiatives. I don't tell Sally about each and every one. I say "can we have a staff meeting about this", and she goes "fine"'. Another teacher similarly commented: 'We are expected to get on and do our own thing, not with her on our back saying "this is what you have got to do now"'.

Teachers have taken up this challenge by leading on a variety of initiatives in school A. One teacher 'revised the year plans and curriculum for each group, and got release time to do it'. Another young teacher was engaged in an action research project on inclusion, which has resulted in changes in school policies. Within the data, there are numerous examples of staff members taking and leading initiatives within or on behalf of the school. The data also revealed that teacher initiative in school A is by no means a purely individual or isolated affair. Teams of four to five teachers have been established to deal with improvement in a variety of areas, such as English and the arts. Teachers who are part of these teams meet to discuss curriculum and teaching and learning issues, and plan and change things when necessary. The English team, for example, produced new exemplar materials for Key Stages 1 and 2, which have been fed back to the rest of the staff. A member of the senior management team is part of each team, but does not lead it.

This commitment to teacher leadership in school A manifests itself in the importance that senior managers in the school attach to teacher decision making and leading initiatives. One teacher was clear on the importance of her involvement in decision making: 'If you've been in the process of getting there, rather than someone just telling you, then that . . . it's a far better way round it, everybody gets more behind it because everybody feels part of the decision making'. Similarly, a member of the senior management team clearly articulated what she saw as the advantages to the school of staff involvement in decision making, namely the wider range of viewpoints that this called upon:

> Having people involved [in decision making] from different backgrounds and different age groups is important, because if you have a head and a deputy who do no or little teaching, they lose touch of what is going on in the classroom, so we're there to say, 'sorry Sally, but that's just not realistic'.

Interestingly, within this school the philosophy of distributed leadership goes well beyond teachers to encompass elements of pupil leadership as well. The school has instituted a strong pupil council. Each class elects representatives who have regular meetings with a member of the senior management team present. Pupils feed back concerns from their peers, bring up issues and are consulted by the senior management team on some matters concerning them. Pupils take this process very seriously, and often lead the meeting themselves without a member of staff facilitating the process.

> Leadership here really goes right the way down, to the youngest Key Stage 1 children, who participate in council meetings and report back – simple things. Recently we had to decide on some furniture to buy for Key Stage 1, and the children had a big say in that. (assistant head)

This amount of involvement was considered to be a way of helping pupils understand that their views were valued and it also allowed the senior management team to communicate directly with pupils about decisions that affected them.

Teacher leadership is clearly a new phenomenon for staff and one that the present head appointed two years ago firmly believes in. The previous head had employed a more traditional, top-down management style that did not involve teachers participating in decision making. When the present head became deputy head, decisions were made still largely by her and the headteacher, without much influence from staff. When appointed as the new head of the school, she also initially employed a more top-down leadership style: She reflects:

> I came into a situation where the results in Key Stage 1 were rock bottom. So when I came in, I initially had to say 'this has got to be done, this has got to be done'. I had to make changes and put things into place very rapidly. This was not my ideal style of leadership, but I saw what had to be done and just had to make them do it . . . but at the same time I have tried to gradually develop leadership skills in everyone. So, the first year I had to come in and broom broom broom, and the second year it was difficult, developing more autonomy among the staff. You don't need to ask me everything, you don't need to ask permission . . . I've read some things about it, and it is true about the letting go, it is about letting go, and as a leader it is quite hard to do that.

From the second year onwards, however, the head recognized the limitations of a 'top-down' approach to leading and started to put in place a more distributed leadership model. This process commenced with the formation of a senior management team that replaced the two-person leadership that had gone before. In addition, new teams were set up to lead specific developments or initiatives within the school consisting largely of teachers but with some senior management presence. Every teacher in the school was also given specific leadership responsibilities, for either academic or pastoral development. These cross-subject teams allowed teachers from different key stages to work together on whole school issues for the first time.

In addition, a new coaching and mentoring programme was introduced to develop the leadership skills of the members of the newly constituted senior management team. This leadership training programme was then extended to all staff. At present, middle-level leaders work as mentors of new staff to help them develop their subject leadership roles. In addition, the school became actively involved with the National College for School Leadership and has been working with other schools as part of the Networked Learning Communities Initiative. This involvement with an external programme has prompted a wide range of new ideas and has given teachers the confidence to lead innovation and change.

Factors supporting teacher leadership

It is clear that the shifting culture over the last two years has contributed significantly to the growth of teacher leadership in school A. The headteacher has deliberately orchestrated a set of opportunities for teachers to lead and has provided the moral support to encourage teachers to take risks. It is also evident that a consistent set of shared values and aims now exists within the school and that these values are reinforced by the head-teacher and her senior management team. All interviewees felt the school now had a strong shared culture that positively encouraged teachers to innovate and lead. As the assistant head commented: 'there is a culture of "we are a team". We work together towards shared aims. So, yes, you can grow and develop, but that's within the interests of the whole school'. Similarly, a subject leader commented: 'we've got the same aims, the same vision, we know why we're here'.

As a consequence of this shared vision, teacher leadership is being facilitated, supported and enhanced within the school. This has meant that teachers have a better understanding of decisions and their implications because they are more involved. It has also ensured that the process of implementation has been stronger because of a collective commitment to the success of new developments. One classroom teacher summarized this by saying, 'I think we talked about what leadership is, what it means. There is a strong philosophy throughout the school that there is an expectation that we take on leadership roles'. This expectation is clearly one of the major contributors to the success of teacher leadership in school A.

Another important element of the school's culture and a key factor in securing successful teacher leadership is trust. As one subject leader said:

> I think trust in this school is very strong, and we've worked hard as a school to develop that. We had a day closure where we talked about building learning communities. We went right back to grass roots and said how do we see learning, and how do we want the school to be managed and led to promote learning?

In this sense, a culture of trust is both a facilitator of and a result of teacher leadership, as giving people autonomy both requires and helps create trust. Another way of actively building trust in school A has been through team-building activities. Last year, for the first time, a team-building day was undertaken, which was commented upon very positively by those interviewed:

> We did a bit of training, which was team building, last year. We did swinging through the trees and stuff, and put people in teams they don't usually work in. The building of the team bit was really important. And it was brilliant, people started to see each other from different points of view, and trust each other more because of that. (member of the senior management team)

While school culture is clearly a strong factor and component in promoting teacher leadership, the evidence shows that there are structural elements that also need to be in place for teacher leadership to work. The establishment of cross-subject teams at school A has proved to be a major way of breaking down subject barriers and boundaries. The fact that all teachers have been given responsibility over a specific area of innovation and development, and are part of subject development teams, meant that the old structural barriers could be crossed:

> The formal school structure isn't really there because everyone has an area of responsibility, alongside their subject. That means that everyone, all teachers, are seen to lead and manage in this school. (member of the senior management team)

This is not to suggest an absence of clear line management structures; in fact, the reverse was true. The teams were confident about reporting lines and where to seek help from members of the senior management team. Although this may seem somewhat contradictory, there was a strong sense among teachers that while they appreciated being involved in leadership, they needed to have a clear view of who to turn to for support when necessary. While everyone is given leadership opportunities at school A, it is clear that there is also some associated expectation, responsibility and accountability. As the assistant head commented, 'I'm not going to give someone a leadership role if they are not going to do anything with it'.

In addition to cultural and structural support, the style and strength of the headteacher and her senior management team was found to be an important contributory factor. The headteacher of school A is considered to be the central driving force behind the success of teacher leadership and development of the school. She has been consistently very supportive of staff, and was described by one member of the senior management team as inspirational: 'In Sally we have an inspirational leader here, who inspires people and people look up to. And teachers, they've got the accountability, but they also want to do it to get Sally's approval, to please Sally, and that is very important too in a leader'.

The teachers feel that good communication with the senior management team is another key factor in the success of teacher leadership at their school. Improving communication is something the members of the senior management team have worked on since the new head was appointed two years ago.

> One thing we've tried to do is to improve communication in the school. So, after every meeting it is my responsibility to go to the two members of staff I'm responsible for and tell them everything that has been said. And that's made a big difference, so everyone knows what's happening now. (members of the senior management team)

There is a culture of open communication at the school and high levels of trust and support among all staff. This has been generated and enhanced by the head and the senior management team by the way they actively support innovation, change and development initiated and led by teachers.

Although relatively few barriers to teacher leadership were identified in the school A, there were one or two issues that staff felt could stand in the way of teachers becoming leaders in school. One barrier mentioned was the willingness of teachers to take on leadership roles. It was posited that some teachers see themselves only as classroom practitioners and therefore could be very reluctant to see themselves in a leadership role or, indeed, to take on such a role. Some teachers simply did not see themselves as being part of school leadership. The head provided the following example:

> One of my staff, she really knows her stuff. But she's always talking about 'they decided, they said', and I want to say, well hang on a minute, it's us. She, like everyone else, gets all the leadership opportunities, but doesn't want to engage unless there is some additional salary point attached. Getting round that is one of my big challenges.

This view was confirmed by one of the teachers: 'I think there are some things that as a staff we can all get involved in, but there's others that I as a teacher don't really want to get involved in because that's the role of the senior management team'. The data suggest that such reluctance is partly due to a lack of confidence about taking on a leadership role and can be overcome with the support of colleagues, but there will inevitably be some teachers who still view leadership as being very little to do with them.

The headteacher also pointed to the some of the difficulties and tensions of distributing leadership within her school: 'Now I'm struggling with having to let go – but you're still the person whose head is on the block when the league tables come out'. The problem of 'letting go' was seen as another potential barrier to distributed forms of leadership in school. The head commented: 'Well, one barrier's got to be, well you have to let go, particularly when you see something happening, and it's not so good, not how you would do it. Do you keep quiet? I guess most of the time you do keep quiet, but it's a bit of an issue for me to let go'. Another barrier concerned the specific set of problems generated by the school within its particular context. As a school in challenging circumstances, distributing leadership is considered to be much more difficult simply because of the tasks facing the head on a daily basis: 'Sometimes, the day-to-day problems, dealing with pupils, parents, the issues that come through the door from the estate, it's mainly single-parent families and so on, can make you lose sight of leadership'.

In summary, school A has made remarkable progress in moving from a top-down autocratic way of leading and managing to a more distributed, democratic form of leadership. This has been achieved through cultural and structural changes together with an emphasis on communication, trust, respect and caring. Within school A, teacher leadership is not merely a particular management style or way of working, but it is fundamental to the vision and culture of the school. Distributed leadership goes beyond staff, and increasingly involves pupils in leadership roles as well. Developing pupils' role as leaders of their own learning is seen by the school as an area that should be developed further.

Much can be learned from school A. As a school in challenging circumstances, it demonstrates that teacher leadership can be both an aspiration and an achievement, even in the face of considerable externally generated difficulties. It shows the importance of the headteacher in creating the conditions within which teacher and student leadership is allowed, enhanced and endorsed. It also reinforces the message that teachers are key to capacity building and that their leadership is more likely to bring about changes that impact positively on teaching and learning. The main challenge for school A will be to sustain this form of leadership over time and to safeguard staff against external pressures that might compete for time, energy and resource. The next chapter looks at a secondary school in which teacher leadership is emerging.

eleven

Emergent teacher leadership

School B

The second case study is of a large secondary school on the outskirts of a city, serving a catchment area consisting largely of council estates. The school's intake is largely from families who are socio-economically disadvantaged. External exam results are relatively poor and, before the present head arrived, the school was in 'special measures', which meant that the school received extra support, but was also officially designated a 'failing school'. At present, the school's exam results are still below the 25 per cent five A–C threshold. The school buildings are currently in a state of disrepair, but a brand new building is being erected on site. The school will move into its new buildings at the start of the next academic year.

In contrast to school A where there was a general consensus that all teachers participated in decision making, this was not the case in school B. Table 7.1 shows that most teachers and managers felt that leadership was shared, but that this was mainly located among senior and middle managers (see p. 76). The vast majority of teachers and managers interviewed said middle managers participated fully in leadership, but this was not the case for ordinary classroom teachers.

The data suggest that middle managers are clearly involved in the process of decision making, and are actively encouraged to become more involved. There is a middle management group, which is consulted on all major decisions, and last year the head 'asked heads of department and heads of year to identify a piece of significant leadership: "What have you done to something that you know has made a difference?".' While attempts are made to distribute leadership beyond the senior management team, it would appear that distributed leadership does not, as yet, extend to other classroom teachers.

In school B teachers felt less likely to initiate decisions than the staff in school A, but the vast majority of staff felt that they were consulted. Within the school, consultation occurs on a range of issues, including school policies, curriculum development and developmental plans. Consultation is very wide-ranging, but teacher involvement in decision making tends to be somewhat limited. Most teachers we interviewed felt that this consultation process was genuine: As one teacher commented: 'They ask us for our opinion ... I do think they actually listen to us'. However, not all staff are happy with the consultation process. As another teacher commented: 'It's a bit of both really, sometimes decisions seem to be made by the senior management team alone, sometimes we are consulted, although I'm not always sure if they take any notice though'.

Many teachers in school B feel able to lead new initiatives and are strongly supported by the senior management team in doing so. All teachers interviewed felt that they received at least some support from the senior management team when embarking upon new initiatives. As one (young) teacher said: 'I think especially at this school they actually work on that. If you're doing extra work, work that'll move the school on, I feel that there is a lot of scope for that sort of thing'. Many examples of teachers leading were mentioned by respondents. For example, a teacher in her first year organized the sports day and a rock-climbing event:

> That is a big initiative for someone in her first year. We didn't say 'ah, you're too young, you can't do this'. We said, 'yeah, ok, but with the right support and guidance'. (assistant head)

Other examples included an initiative by the head of modern foreign languages to introduce a new set of methods to improve pupils' communication skills in foreign languages, and a maths teacher who had worked with colleagues to rewrite all the maths schemes in the department to fit in with the National Numeracy Strategy. These opportunities for teacher initiative and leadership were seen to make school B different from other secondaries in the local education authority. These schools were seen to be managed in a more 'top-down' way with less scope for initiative.

Teacher leadership is very positively viewed within school B. Both managers and teachers said they thought it could make a positive contribution to school improvement. In the words of one teacher: 'You're getting more involved, more people are giving ideas, more people are getting valued, so yes, definitely, it will help the school'. Overall, while there is clear management support for teacher leadership, and taking initiative is encouraged, involvement in decision making tends to be limited to middle management.

In school B it is clear that distributed leadership is emerging, but it is certainly much less developed than in school A. It is also clear that the school has made some progress towards teacher leadership when compared with the leadership style that had operated there before. Under the previous head, leadership was largely autocratic and top-down. The present head has started to devolve leadership, supported by most members of the senior management team. As one head of department put it: 'Since the new senior management came in ... as a staff we're much more involved with everything that's happened, we've much more influence over what has happened. We have meetings where we have input into things'. This process has been incremental: 'Increasingly, as the school has developed, as middle managers have learnt to become leaders, they are getting more autonomy', according to the assistant head we interviewed.

The senior management team as a whole, rather than the head alone, is seen as having moved the school in the direction of greater distributed leadership. By setting up a middle management committee, attempts have been formally made to encourage teacher initiative. In addition, there have been widespread consultation meetings about major policy decisions involving all staff.

Factors promoting teacher leadership

As in school A, school culture at school B is considered to be a key element in securing increased teacher leadership. School B has a very collegial culture that promotes the sharing of good practice. This collegial culture is considered to exist across the school, and not just to reside within the senior and middle management teams. Collegiality is seen as being central to school improvement at school B and a main driver of change. As the head said:

> There's a difference, isn't there, between collegiality and conviviality. I've worked in places where people are terribly matey, and we buy each other cream buns and go for drinks, but having a climate where people can be critical of each other, hold each other to account is different.

As highlighted earlier, a shared vision would seem to be a key component of successful teacher leadership. Most respondents saw this shared vision as part of the culture of school B. As a middle manager said, 'We are all very aware of where the school is going, we were consulted on the strategic plan, and we know we are responsible in our particular area to help the school meet its vision'.

Structural changes have also contributed to the generation of teacher leadership. All teachers interviewed felt positive about the fact that the present management team had instituted regular whole-staff meetings, which are used as key arenas for consultation. As the assistant head said: 'The head is always saying: "get back to me, scribble on these notes, let me know what you think"'. There are also regular meeting with heads of department, heads of year and the middle management team as a whole, where shared decision making is encouraged. The opportunity to have an input at these meeting is appreciated by teachers. The fortnightly line management meetings, where line managers sit down with the staff they have line management responsibility over and discuss any upcoming initiatives and invite feedback, are also seen as a way of distributing leadership.

Clear line management structures are also seen to be important, as in school A. Teachers felt they could talk to a member of the senior management team about the initiatives they were leading. Some teachers viewed the professional development opportunities they had as being critical to enhancing their confidence to lead. Another factor that was seen to be important in generating teacher leadership was the opportunity for internal promotion within the school:

> We are quite lucky in that there is quite a lot of internal promotion at this school. If they like you, they'll try and keep you by giving you leadership opportunities. (maths teacher)

Many of the young teachers interviewed in this school are highly ambitious, and promotion is clearly a major motivator for them.

Support from school management at all levels (senior and departmental) is another key factor in encouraging teacher leadership at the school. As one teacher said, 'We have to go through the hierarchy, we bring an idea to the line manager, who'll say yea or nay, but my line manager is great, she's been really supportive'. Senior management also monitors and directs the work of teachers, but this is becoming less important as teachers become more confident in taking on leadership.

Some barriers to teacher leadership were identified in school B. The first of these was lack of time. School B is a challenging school, which, as prior research has shown, means that teachers have to work generally much harder than teachers in less challenging ones.

> That's obviously one thing that hinders you in taking up your leadership role ... if you are spending a lot of time dealing with difficult children, then you have less time to do interesting initiatives and all the lovely things. (teacher)

A lack of experience and confidence on the part of teachers was also identified as a potential barrier. School B has quite a young staff, and many of the older members of staff have not worked in an environment in which they were asked to take on leadership roles before. Suspicion and a lack of confidence were considered to be barriers that would prove difficult to overcome. Within school B, a minority of staff tended to be viewed as somewhat apathetic, and unwilling to take on leadership roles or offer feedback when consulted. While most teachers want to get involved in leadership, some one intimidated by colleagues who are less than supportive about taking a leadership role.

Another barrier identified in school B was the fact that not all senior managers were equally responsive to teacher initiative and involvement in decision making. Some teachers commented that they didn't feel they were always listened to when consulted, and that some managers still prefer a 'top-down' leadership style. 'At the end of the day we do take the decision. At the end of the day it's our responsibility. We would be shirking our responsibility if we didn't take the decisions' (deputy head). Occasionally, communications between senior management and staff are seen as problematic: 'sometimes, decisions are taken, and the reasons are not communicated to us. If we were informed a little bit more, everything would be fine, I think' (head of year 7).

Finally, the fact that school B is below the 25 per cent five A–C threshold is seen as invoking particular tensions and problems:

> When you're in the situation we are, just out of serious weaknesses, with poor exam results still, below the magical 25 per cent five A* to Cs that the DfES want, your accountability is extreme ... The earned autonomy thing, it's not helpful. I believe it should be reversed – all schools have autonomy until they get themselves into serious difficulties. (headteacher)

Before joining the school, the head had previously been at a school in an affluent area of the county. In that school, distributed leadership had been practised for a long time, and the head initially wished to do the same in his new school. However, in contrast to his previous school, school B was a failing school that needed to be 'turned round' quickly so that it could be removed from 'special measures': 'I felt in that situation I had to change my leadership style, and become much less democratic'. Changing styles back again towards more democratic forms of leadership has been a challenge and a challenge he feels is still ongoing. It is clear that the wider educational context and its associated demands can place schools under pressure and actively prevent distributed forms of leadership.

In summary, the head of school B is clearly committed to developing more distributed and democratic leadership in his school, and most teachers interviewed also share this commitment to the principles of teacher leadership. Moving from a 'top-down' style of leadership to a more distributed form of leadership is proving challenging. However, it is clear that the school has made significant progress in this direction. Almost all respondents agreed that leadership was not merely a matter of the senior management team imposing its views and policies, but that it should be shared more widely with middle management. Classroom teachers are not yet strongly involved, although they are encouraged to take initiative in a variety of areas.

The movement towards teacher leadership is clearly moving at a slower pace than in school A. It is possible that continuing professional development a more proactive policy geared towards developing leadership skills, such as that implemented in school A, would help alleviate this problem. Similarly, providing more specific leadership responsibilities to all members of staff, in particular through the use of school development teams in different (curriculum) areas, could provide staff with leadership experience.

It will be interesting to see how school B develops in the coming years, particularly with a move to a new school building. The potential for teacher leadership is certainly present in the school and is slowly being realized. The increased morale that may come with the move to new premises could strengthen that process further.

twelve

Restricted teacher leadership

School C

The third case study is of a comprehensive school located in the leafy commuter belt of a large city. The school serves an affluent community and there are few socio-economic problems in the area. Housing around the school consist largely of private dwellings. However, despite these circumstances, not all teachers feel that parents strongly support the school and their children's education. Parents were described by interviewees as 'self-made' people, who saw their children's education as the role of the school, rather than something they had to get involved in themselves. Interestingly, the school is viewed by parents as 'under-performing' and consequently not the first-choice school for parents in the community. This had led to the school being under-subscribed over several years. Under the previous head, school performance had improved significantly, though it was still considered to be an under-performing school.

In contrast to schools A and B where there is a clear consensus on the extent to which teachers are involved in decision making (i.e. all staff in school A and middle managers in school B), this is clearly not the case in school C. Respondents are fairly divided on this issue, as can be seen in Table 7.1 (see p. 76).

It would appear that while teachers do not participate in decision making at the whole-school level, some departments have developed strategies to encourage teacher leadership in their departments. One head of department in particular strongly encouraged teacher leadership:

> Everyone in the department is given something to look at, something the department needs, or they need or are good at. For example, one member of staff is looking at questioning. He is going into classrooms, and seeing how others do it ... then they discuss with who they have observed what they have seen. Then that is discussed in the department, and disseminated. They take the lead on how that is done, they lead on it.

Involvement in leadership at the whole-school level was seen by some interviewees to be limited to the senior management team, although others felt that middle leaders were involved. As in school B, teachers tended to be consulted on decisions, rather than being given the opportunity to instigate ideas. However, the data revealed that views on this were again somewhat mixed. As one middle-level leader said: 'Teachers have the opportunity to have their voice heard, but whether staff would agree their voice is heard enough is open to debate'.

Teachers at school C do see some scope for taking initiative, and have done so on a number of occasions. For example, the literacy coordinator is pursuing the purchase of mini whiteboards for the school, while another teacher decided the school would take part in the 'World Challenge', which had never been done before. However, relatively few examples of teacher leadership tended to be forthcoming in comparison with schools A and B.

It would appear that teacher leadership is not particularly developed in this school, but interestingly this does not seem to be the result of a lack of support for the idea from the head. On the contrary, the head of school C expressed strong support for distributed and democratic forms of leadership, and had clearly thought about leadership styles and approaches. In particular, empowering teachers was an aspect he considered to be very important to the effectiveness of the school:

> If you disempower teachers, you actually end up creating in the school a blame culture, where people just look around for other people to poke when things go wrong. So what I wanted to do was to set up a culture that empowered people.

These positive views were echoed by other staff members in the school. The head of the science department, for example, stated:

> I think to be satisfied in their job, people need to experience achievement. They need to grow professionally. Teacher leadership does that for them. A lot of people want financial rewards or status, but the self-respect you get from being better at your job than you were last year is the key, I believe.

This view was also reflected by a school governor, who said: 'I think it's important that people believe they have something to contribute to any organization, be it school or British Rail or whatever'. Teacher leadership, therefore, is supported across the school as a concept, but the extent to which it operates in practice is limited.

Within school C, the support for teacher leadership expressed by the head and middle-level leaders did mean that certain initiatives were being undertaken. Before the current head joined the school, few new initiatives were being instigated or implemented at the school. As the leadership style of the previous head was generally quite hierarchical, initiatives were encouraged as long as they did not interfere with senior management policies and aims. The head of science, for example, is a strong supporter of teacher leadership and has tried to develop this in her department. With support from the Cambridge Learning Partnership, she has tried to develop the leadership capacities of her staff.

> I was introduced to the concept of teacher leadership through the work we are doing with Cambridge, and have tried to develop this in my department, giving everyone the opportunity to lead on something. Some teachers are better at it than others, but overall it has been very successful, and is something I want to continue developing, at this school or somewhere else.

The present head has also tried to encourage teacher leadership, in his view, largely by attempting to change the culture. Creating a blame-free culture is seen as particularly important by the head: 'I talk to staff a lot about blame . . . I emphasize that blame absorbs energy'. The head has also tried to emphasize middle-level leaders' and teachers' freedom to take decisions:

> I talk a lot about the Toyota model. Toyota being the biggest car company in the world. They have localized ordering systems. They don't have a universal ordering system. We use the same idea here. Yes, we have some global aims, some goals for the school, but how you do that in science is not down to me, it's down to the scientists, they know their subject.

While support for teacher leadership is strong in school C, it does not appear to be permeating beyond the senior management team. The reasons why teacher leadership is not as widespread as in schools A and B chiefly reside in the culture of the school. A key difference between this school and schools A and B is that the cultural and structural changes required to support teacher leadership have not been put in place. One teacher mentioned school culture as being an enhancing factor: 'it's a very, sort of, open school. And there isn't a very strong hierarchical thing, it doesn't feel like that anyway. You feel like you have a voice and your ideas are valid, but I can't think of anything specific, really'.

Structures, which were important factors in schools A and B, were hardly mentioned as an enhancing factor or a barrier in school C. The only facilitating factor to broker leadership was highlighted by one individual as the opportunity for staff to engage in professional development:

> There is a wide range of opportunities that people have to go on training to become better leaders. For instance, at the moment there is an initiative, which is being run by Cambridge University, which is specifically this, it's a leadership course. This year, two members of staff are involved in this. People could buy in, actually volunteer to go into that. Having said that, we are also targeting a few people who we thought could benefit from that. (continuing professional development coordinator)

In relation to the provision of high-quality continuing professional development, the headteacher reflected upon the increased confidence that staff have developed due to the improved performance of the school. His view was that this factor would make them more confident in taking on leadership roles. Conversely, the continuing professional development coordinator felt that if staff wanted to take on leadership roles, they needed to be supported by the senior management team: 'If people want to do something, a lot of support is given to them'. One middle-level leader, who is involved in the Cambridge project and was one of the instigators of teacher leadership in the school, felt that there was insufficient impetus and support for teachers to be leaders within the school.

Barriers to teacher leadership

There were a number of barriers to teacher leadership that were highlighted in school C. The main barrier, despite his obvious support for teacher leadership, is perceived to be the leadership of the head. The headteacher is seen as a weak leader by several teachers, which is, in turn, seen as a major barrier to the development of teacher leadership. This perceived lack of leadership from the centre has meant that teachers are often not sure what they are supposed to do.

> People have to come forward, because they are not getting a nudge from the head. It is my personal opinion that you have to ask staff, approach them, say 'are *you* interested'. Given a little bit of support, and a little bit of a nudge, they will take things on. But they are not being nudged. (middle manager)

Many teachers also feel that roles, including leadership roles, are not clearly defined in the school, makes many teachers reticent in taking on leadership responsibilities:

> I think if roles were more clearly defined, then it would be easier. You sometimes get the impression you can do something, and then someone will say, 'oh no, you shouldn't have done that'. Or you'll think, 'I can't do that, 'cos somebody will say something, and then they'll be "oh, why didn't you do that"'. (teacher)

Another key barrier concerns the lack of communication from the head and the senior management team:

> Communication . . . I think most people here would say that's an issue. It's not brilliant. I think most people would say its a bit last-minute, or that you are communicated with verbally, but sometimes you want things on paper. (literacy coordinator)

Teachers felt that the head was not communicating his vision of teacher leadership clearly enough. The head of science said: 'I think the head would like to have everyone involved, but there is a big difference with the reality. I don't think he has communicated his vision clearly enough'. A governor put it more bluntly:

> Who participates in leadership? The head doesn't participate much in leadership in this school. There's a lot of talk about it, and one criticism – the only criticism – I had of the previous head was that she did disenfranchise the middle . . . but now staff, at the middle and at the bottom, are just confused.

While many teachers feel that the main impediment to the development of teacher leadership in school C resides with the leadership of the headteacher, the head himself saw teacher attitudes as a key barrier. Teachers, in his view, did not necessarily want to take ownership or leadership responsibilities. For example, the head felt that attempts to devolve ownership for behaviour management strategies to teachers had been rebuffed: 'behaviour management is an example where teachers were given ownership but simply handed it back saying tell us what to do'. Some teachers are seen as cynical by the head: 'There's always those people who have got themselves into a very cynical way of thinking. I think it's important to tackle those people, and tell them it's not all about cynicism in this job'. Others want remuneration for their leadership efforts: 'What I hear a lot is that they want to get paid if it's something extra . . . what I want to move towards is a culture where teachers lead because they want to lead'.

Another important barrier, as in all the case study schools, was a lack of time, which impedes staff from taking initiatives:

> Time is obviously one thing that hinders you in taking up your leadership role ... if you are spending all your time dealing with day-to-day things, then you have less time to do initiatives and stuff. (teacher)

In addition, school C has suffered from high staff turnover, which again has proved to be a major barrier to developing school-wide leadership:

> You often end up with transient teams. How do you create a team, when your department has turned over twelve members of staff in the past two years? (head)

A number of cultural barriers at school C were also considered to be impediments to teacher leadership. The main barriers identified were a lack of a shared vision and lack of a collaborative culture within the school. As noted in the previous case studies, a shared vision is crucial to the success of teacher leadership in any school. However, in the views of many respondents, this element is lacking in school C:

> I think in this school what needs to be established at the moment is a much clearer vision of where the school is going. Maybe not everybody is sure of what the vision is, and people have different interpretations of it. (continuing professional development coordinator)

> A first thing that really needs to be established is a clear vision – where we want to go, what we want to be and achieve for those children. What sort of adults we want them to become. And in the end you've got to have someone – that's why we pay the head an inordinate sum of money – to do that role. (governor)

Teachers at school C frequently mentioned a lack of clear and shared vision, which exacerbated problems with communication. The central problem at school C, it would appear, is the prevalence of a 'non-collaborative culture': 'We're not very good at working together for the same thing, the same goals. We tend to operate in bubbles' (literacy coordinator). What initiatives are taken are often taken individually or within a department, without recourse to the school as a whole. 'One problem is that I perceive things as whole school initiatives, but they're not, really. They're someone's baby, and I find it very hard not to start muddling with someone else's baby' (head of science). Some teachers who have leadership roles feel isolated because they are not part of a formal team: 'I'm not part of the leadership team; in fact, I'm not a part of a team at all' (literacy coordinator). Integrating non-traditional leadership roles into the school structure was shown to be an important issue in preventing teacher leadership from spreading.

There is a sense in which teachers at school C have not yet taken on board risk taking and do not trust each other:

> What we need, but we are not there yet, is to develop a culture of risk taking, and if they do take a risk and it goes pear-shaped, say, 'ok, that's the learning process' . . . It's like in the classroom, if a kid gets something wrong, we don't batter them over it, we say, 'ok, what did you learn from that'. (head)

The fact that this risk-taking culture is not present has made teachers reticent in coming forwards with new ideas and initiatives.

In summary, the main message about teacher leadership emanating from school C is that sheer commitment to the idea in itself will not result in change within the organization. In other words, simply being signed up to the idea of teacher leadership does not mean it will take place. Teacher leadership needs to be facilitated and embraced as a cultural norm within the school. While the head is showing a clear intellectual commitment to distributed leadership in the school, this in itself is insufficient to make it happen. Most teachers do not feel involved in decision making and, consequently, remain disenfranchised from leadership.

This case study reinforces the importance of three key factors in generating and supporting teacher leadership. These factors are: a shared vision and positive school culture; high levels of trust; and clear communication and structural support for teacher leadership. All three case studies have reiterated the importance of teacher leadership as a cultural norm and the need for support from the headteacher and senior management team. From these case studies, and more broadly the findings of the GTC/NUT research project, there are important lessons about initiating, developing and sustaining teacher leadership. The next chapter considers the key messages about nurturing teacher leadership in schools.

Part 4

Future directions for teacher leadership

thirteen

Nurturing teacher leadership

The three studies described in the previous chapters highlight varying degrees of teacher leadership in action. They point to some of the benefits of teachers collaborating in a productive way, together with some of the key conditions or requirements for making this happen in practice. This chapter reflects upon the main findings from the cases and attempts to distil the key messages about initiating, developing and enhancing teacher leadership

A deliberate process

It is clear from all the case studies that for teacher leadership to be successful, it has to be a carefully orchestrated and deliberate process. The case studies showed that where it was most effective, teacher leadership had been carefully put in place through changing structures and culture in a strategic way. The data revealed that for teacher leadership to be successful, there needs to be a fundamental cultural shift in the vision and values of the organization. It requires staff to understand and want to engage in leadership activities. Viewing teacher leadership as yet another initiative alongside others or as something that is the preserve of a few enthusiasts in the school is unlikely to work. Teacher leadership needs to be deeply embedded in the culture of the school. In those schools visited where teacher leadership was embedded, it had become a part of the school mission and culture and permeated everything the school did. Teachers and senior managers at these schools used terms like 'creating a democratic school' and 'a school as a learning organization' to describe this process.

In the majority of schools in the GTC/NUT study, teacher leadership had been prompted by a new headteacher who had taken the decision to distribute leadership. However, the extent to which teachers felt able to participate in leadership activities varied considerably from school to school. In some schools, the headteacher had met with resistance from other members of the senior management team and from teachers when introducing the idea. In those schools where teacher leadership has not been successfully established, teacher apathy tended to be identified as a root cause. Wasley (1991) noted that resistance to leading arises from teachers lacking understanding, support or reward for their additional efforts. This study concluded that for teacher leadership to become reality, teachers must be given real support for their work. Consequently, it is important that teachers are both willing and sufficiently skilled to take on leadership roles. This implies a time and resource investment to ensure they are prepared to lead.

It is also important that once teachers are given leadership responsibility, it is not taken back from them should things go wrong. The principle of 'no-blame innovation' is of central importance here. If teachers are to lead innovation and change, then it is inevitable that, at times, mistakes will be made. How these mistakes are responded to by the headteacher and senior management team will be critically important. Simply removing leadership from them will cause teachers to feel their trust has been betrayed. For example, one of the headteachers of the schools in this study had taken back leadership responsibilities from teachers when the school received poorer than expected results (the school served a highly socio-economically deprived community). This action led to a large number of teachers leaving the school, an atmosphere of mistrust emerged and a flat refusal by teachers to engage fully in any proposed reforms. The school's exam scores declined further and the headteacher resigned soon after. In such circumstances, it will be almost impossible to re-introduce distributed forms of leadership as trust has been lost. Consequently, distributing leadership has to be carefully handled and managed. It is a process of cultural change that demands consistency of vision and a high degree of commitment from teachers to make it work.

Networking

The case studies revealed a wide variation of networking activity that constituted teacher leadership. They showed that teacher leadership often occurred within a variety of formal and informal collaborative settings. In England, the changing educational climate towards federations, partnerships and networks has afforded more opportunities for teachers to collaborate and has provided a renewed legitimacy for teacher collaboration.

Four of the schools visited were involved in external initiatives or programmes aimed at promoting collaboration. Two were involved in 'Networked Learning Communities' (NLC), one in 'Improving the Quality of Education for All' (IQEA) and one in 'Best Practice Networks' (Specialist Schools Trust). These initiatives had prompted new groupings among teachers both within and across schools, which were predominantly subject-based or were action research groups with a mandate to undertake developments or to problem solve in certain key areas for the school or schools.

However, it was not the case that the impetus towards collaboration and networking had come from participation in externally driven initiatives in all case study schools. In some schools the drivers were internal, and often informal. In particular, as we saw in the examples of the teacher team working to improve English and the arts in one school, teachers themselves, with the encouragement of senior managers, had formed school improvement groupings.

A number of advantages of networking have been summarized recently by Hargreaves (2004). He suggests that teachers should collaborate and innovate because:

- Teachers do it anyway. As teachers adjust materials or ways of organizing lessons to help pupils learn, their improvisations are a form of innovation. *Without this creative capacity to innovate, a teacher does not succeed in the profession.*
- Innovation is essential to improving one's professional skills and to adapting to meet changing circumstances. *Innovation is a way of learning professionally.*
- Innovation empowers staff and is highly rewarding professionally. *To see how being creative and innovative makes a difference for pupils is one of the joys of teaching.*
- In our knowledge-based economy, students need to be innovative to succeed at work and in life. *When staff actively model innovative behaviour in school, students learn why innovation matters and is something they can do too.*

He also suggests that teachers should network:

- To transform schools so that there is yet better teaching and learning, teachers must work smarter, not harder. *Today, most innovation is the activity of networked teams, not individuals.*
- To share good practice and transfer it rapidly. *Lateral networks do this more effectively than top-down hierarchies.*
- Government needs to empower teachers to use their creativity in the task of transformation. Networks of peers feed the creative co-production of new knowledge that is the source of better professional practice and

renewed professional pride. *A key to successful innovation is therefore combining innovation with networks.*

The case studies reveal that teacher leadership provides the infrastructure for promoting innovation and for maximizing networking and collaboration both within and between schools.

Staff development and external support

One problem in developing teacher leadership is that staff lack confidence and in some cases leadership skills to perform the roles and responsibilities. This is not to suggest that they are incapable of becoming leaders, as much research has shown that leadership can to a large extent be learned and developed (Muijs and Harris 2003). However, it is clear that leadership development requires strong support and specific forms of professional development of staff.

In some schools in the study, leadership development had been encouraged by sending teachers on local education authority (LEA) leadership courses, or having in-house INSET delivery on leadership development. While undoubtedly useful, these traditional forms of professional development are by no means the only, or necessarily the most useful, way of developing leadership capability. In the most successful schools in our sample, innovative staff development methods were being used to develop leadership and collaborative skills. For example, mentoring or coaching was used in a number of the schools to great effect, as was shadowing in one school visited. The key point is that some form of professional development needs to be in place to equip teachers to lead effectively.

External support is also important in helping schools develop teacher leadership. The schools in the study that had received strong support from the LEA in developing teacher leaders, or which were part of a collaborative network in which teacher leadership was stressed, clearly found it easier to develop this form of leadership in their schools. The support provided through university partnerships also proved to be a key factor in helping three schools develop teacher leadership. The emphasis upon collaboration in these schools meant that teachers were encouraged to share ideas and to problem solve together. The study found that teachers felt that this way of working together would help generate a collective creativity that was both innovative and rewarding. The innovative work in most of the case study schools had resulted from the work of groups rather than individuals.

Where schools were part of externally facilitated networks, teachers had more opportunities to meet with other teachers both from their own and other schools. The provision of specific resources and, not least, time to engage in collaboration were clearly facilitating factors, which allowed teachers to develop innovative practices. The generation of shared knowledge that was evident in those schools that were part of professional networks such as Networked Learning Communities is another advantage of collaborative action.

School culture and school structures

As mentioned earlier, school culture and structure are key elements in allowing teacher leadership to flourish. The supportive, no-blame culture we found in the successful case study schools was clearly one of the reasons for the development of teachers as leaders there. This supportive culture rests both on supportive and clear structures, and a strong element of trust.

It is also clear that teacher leadership operates best where there are high degrees of trust. However, trust needs to work both ways. Teachers need to trust the motives of senior management, which can sometimes be construed as taking advantage by asking teachers to do more.

Developing trust is therefore a key task within a school, in which communication also plays an important role. Trust is most likely to develop in schools were relationships are strong, in the sense that staff know, or think they know, one another (Bryk and Schneider, 2003). This means that constant interaction, rather than a more distant style of leadership, as found in case study school C, is likely to facilitate trust. As well as being an important element in developing teacher leadership, involving teachers in leadership, especially where this takes the form of collaborative teams and action, can help develop trust, as it allows positive relationships to develop.

While a shared culture and goals are an important prerequisite to distributing leadership in a school, teacher leadership itself impacts upon the culture of the school. In many cases, the study showed that school goals and policies were arrived at through a process of consultation, through working groups and teacher involvement. The involvement of teachers in decision making on crucial as well as on less central issues, helps create a shared feeling of responsibility for the goals of the organization and a shared sense of direction.

The importance of shared goals highlights the need to coordinate the various areas of activity or the developmental work within the school. In some schools, this was achieved by regular meetings between the working groups and the senior management team. In these meetings, updates on progress were provided and any resource issues discussed. In addition, the senior management team in each school carefully monitored the work of the groups and considered engaging in external initiatives only if this complemented their work. For example, one school became involved in Networked Learning Communities simply because it reinforced what they were already doing.

It is not surprising that in the schools where teacher leadership had been most successfully introduced, attempts had been made to provide recognition and rewards for teachers' efforts, either informally or formally. In some schools, efforts had been made to turn leadership into formal roles through enhanced promotion opportunities. In all cases, teachers' work was formally recognized by being disseminated throughout the school, highlighting the important contribution teachers made. External accreditation was also an option at certain schools and teachers generally agreed that they found this an incentive.

In summary, developing teacher leadership is not an easy process. It is closely related to re-culturing, as it means a fundamental shift in the purposes and practices of the school. There are several conclusions that can be drawn from this study. The first is that beliefs matter. Common or shared beliefs permeate the culture of the school and in many ways define it. Secondly, structures matter. Structures can negate or support a culture of collaboration. They can divide cultures if boundaries are drawn too closely. Thirdly, trust matters. Without trust between teachers it is unlikely that positive collaboration or mutual development will occur. Finally, rewards matter. Whether intrinsic or extrinsic, teachers need to feel that their work is recognized and that there is some acknowledgement of their achievements within or on behalf of the school.

In the schools visited, teacher leadership varied considerably because of differences in culture, structure, trust and reward. In the most successful cases where teacher leadership was fully implemented, it was seen as contributing to school improvement by both teachers and senior managers. In other schools where teacher leadership was not well established, school improvement was more difficult to locate. The next chapter will explore the relationship between teacher leadership and school improvement in some depth.

fourteen

Improving schools through teacher leadership

Introduction

It has been suggested that the time is 'ripe for exploring new ways in which to increase teachers' professional knowledge and skill' (Hargreaves 2004). The government's 'Transformation Agenda' suggests that improvement should be faster and undertaken in a way that allows innovation to flourish. There are many drivers identified for this deep level change, but in summary there is a general recognition that the recent improvement strategies and initiatives between 1997 and 2002 (National Numeracy Strategy, National Literacy Strategy) have inevitable limitations and that new approaches to improvement are required. It has been shown that the rate of improvement has been 'levelling off' and that the amount of improvement secured by any single strategy has been relatively modest.

The evaluation evidence from New American Schools (NAS) formed in 1991 to create and develop whole-school approaches to school improvement has similarly pointed towards the limitations of externally driven reform packages to impact positively on teaching and learning. These whole-school approaches were led by a 'design team', a group that conceives of the reform design, engineers the principles, implementation strategy and/or the materials to accompany the reform; and often provides support to local schools and local education authorities (districts) in the form of training. Design teams come in a variety of forms and serve different functions. Within NAS, they included 'Success for All', 'Coalition of Essential Schools' and the Comer Development Programme. In the UK, design teams would include 'Improving the Quality of Education for All' and 'The High Reliability Project'. Unlike the USA, there has not been a massive investment at the government level in supporting externally designed school improvement efforts. Therefore, the empirical evidence about the effectiveness of these programmes remains limited.

In contrast, in the USA, New American Schools has involved more than 4000 schools using seven different design programmes. The evaluation report, however, states that the 'initial hypothesis, that, by adopting a whole school design a school could improve its performance, was largely unproven' (Berends *et al.* 2002: 37) In general, the evaluation concludes that in those schools where implementation of the designs was initially high (over a four year period), subsequently implementation weakened and outcomes decreased. In short, the NAS initiative was an experimental approach to school reform that highlights the difficulties of initiating and disseminating large-scale educational improvement.

Datnow *et al.* (2003: 39) suggest that 'all change is local' and question the proposition that models developed in one school can be successfully transported to other schools with entirely different teacher and student compositions. While some reform design teams market their approaches on the basis that they can be implemented in any school, at any time, in reality the context is important for school reform. One of the most consistent findings that emanates from the research literature is the degree of variability due to local circumstances and contextual differences. It shows that the variability in implementation is often due to local contextual demands, constraints or differences. School improvement is rarely a linear, rational process where programmes are uniformly or fully implemented. Even where programmes or policies are relatively straightforward, their implementation can be very different across localities, schools and classrooms (Elmore and Sykes 1992).

When reform fails, the technical rational perspective, which dominates the design and implementation process, places the blame on those teachers, schools or LEAs that did not implement the model successfully. What is rarely questioned is whether the reform or innovation was appropriate to the needs of particular schools, in particular contexts, with particular types of pupils. Where reform succeeds, the evidence suggests that the implementation process involves an active and dynamic interaction between local educators and those driving the reform. In other words, reform is a two-way process between developers and local educators, which allows context to be considered and factored into the implementation process.

It is increasingly clear that successful reform and school improvement efforts involve mutual adaptation and are co-constructed. As Datnow *et al.* (2003: 44) point out, in the

> grammar of co-construction the causal arrow of change travels in multiple directions among active participants in all domains of the

> system over time. This grammar makes the reform process flexible with people who have different intentions/interests and interpretations and who enter into the process at different points along the (reform) course. Thus many actors negotiate with and adjust to one another within and across contexts.

The central message, therefore, is that 'context matters when studying school level reforms' and when considering alternative approaches to school improvement and change. As Desimone (2000) found in a review of comprehensive school reform, only a few studies have actually examined the contextual variables that influence the implementation process. Datnow *et al.* (2003: 60) offer the following guidelines for action in placing reform in the local context:

(a) view context and the diversity of the language, race, class and gender of those involved as a strength to build upon;
(b) approach schools with flexibility and develop a set of strategies for attending to local conditions;
(c) see teachers as an asset and as collaborators, not uninformed obstacles or passive implementers of reform;
(d) address the cultural and political dimensions of change, not just the technical dimension;
(e) include equity as an explicit goal in their reforms.

This chapter considers how teachers can be collaborators in the reform or improvement process. It considers how teachers can be agents of change, lead change and, most importantly, how this can be best facilitated and supported.

The teacher leader and school improvement

Despite a growing research base on teacher leadership, there are still questions about whether and how they contribute to school improvement, particularly within the current context of externally prescribed initiatives and reforms. To address this question, we first need to look at what the research base tells us about successful school improvement and the place of teachers as leaders within improvement processes. The literature shows that even though there are differences of approach, highly effective school improvement projects have been found to share certain characteristics or features. A broad comparative analysis of highly successful programmes demonstrates a number of shared principles or features (Harris 2000b). This analysis found that effective school improvement programmes:

- focus closely on classroom improvement;

- utilize discrete instructional or pedagogical strategies – that is, they are explicit in the models of teaching they prescribe;
- apply pressure at the implementation stage to ensure adherence to the programme;
- collect systematic evaluative evidence about the impact upon schools and classrooms;
- mobilize change at a number of levels within the organization (e.g. classroom, department, teacher level);
- generate cultural as well as structural change;
- engage teachers in professional dialogue and development;
- provide external agency and support.

Although school improvement programmes and projects vary in terms of content, nature and approach, they reflect a similar philosophy. Central to this philosophy is an adherence to the school as the centre of change and the teacher as the catalyst for classroom change and development. Within highly effective school improvement programmes, there are non-negotiable elements:

- a central focus on teaching and learning;
- a commitment to meaningful professional development;
- distributed forms of (teacher) leadership.

Even though new school improvement projects and initiatives appear to emerge daily, evidence concerning their impact is not always forthcoming. Critics of the school improvement field have highlighted the relative absence of evaluative evidence regarding the impact of school improvement upon student performance and achievement. In addition, there has been little consideration of the relative effectiveness of different school improvement initiatives in enhancing student performance. The studies that do exist offer little evidence of the relative effectiveness of one approach over another.

Further comparative studies of school improvement are needed to assist schools in selecting improvement programmes that are most effective and 'fit' their developmental needs. At present, there is an accumulating knowledge base about school improvement arising from the numerous projects and programmes around the world. This knowledge base provides important insights into the process of improvement and there are several common components of successful school improvement:

1. *Vision building.* Many school improvement projects require schools to share in a vision of where the school could be, or to generate their own vision with support and help from external agents. There is evidence to suggest that the possibilities for school improvement are extended if there is a clear vision linked to high-quality support. It also suggests

that this vision needs to be shared and regularly reconfirmed as the process of change takes place. Conversely, the absence of a clear vision has been shown to lead to confusion, demoralization and failure within much school improvement work.

2. *Extended leadership*. At the core of any school improvement effort is a new way of teachers and management working together. In schools engaged in school improvement, both senior managers and teachers have to function as leaders and decision makers as they try to bring about fundamental changes. Essentially, school improvement requires a re-conceptualization of leadership whereby teachers and managers engage in shared decision making and risk taking. The emphasis is upon active and participatory leadership in school improvement work, rather than top-down delegation.
3. *Programme fit*. Many different programmes for school improvement exist, but there is no one 'blueprint for action'. The research shows that there is no universal starting point for any school. In each individual school context, history, leadership, staffing, incentives and personal history will vary. All these factors play an important role in school improvement and highlight the need to select the school improvement programme that best 'fits' the individual school. However, in most cases schools choose programmes without consideration or knowledge of the alternatives.
4. *Focus on students*. What distinguishes the school improvement movement from other school reform efforts is the understanding that it is necessary to focus upon student outcomes in academic performance as the key success criterion, rather than teacher perceptions of the innovation. Highly successful school improvement projects have been shown to place an 'emphasis upon specific learning outcomes rather than general learning goals' (Hopkins 2001: 231). Where school improvement works most effectively, it involves teachers aiming for a clearly defined set of learning outcomes or targets. Within successful school improvement, the learning level is the main focus for development and change. Hence, within successful projects there is an emphasis upon well-defined student learning outcomes, together with the provision of clear instructional frameworks.
5. *Multi-level intervention*. Much early school improvement work tended to concentrate on school-level change. However, subsequent work has recognized the importance of encouraging change at the level of the school, teacher and classroom. Consequently, a multi-level approach is now part of the most effective school improvement programmes. This necessitates using all initiators, promoters and activists within the change process at all levels, both externally and internally.
6. *Instructionally driven*. Within a number of highly effective school

improvement projects, there is a clear articulation of the instructional framework that guides the development activity at the classroom level. In Success For All, for example, the instructional framework comes from the research base on cooperative learning. A range of classroom strategies are used within the project, such as 'think pair share' and 'peer tutoring', both directly derived from the cooperative learning literature. In IQEA, Joyce's (1992) models of teaching provide the cornerstone for the developmental work in schools. Schools are encouraged to work on one model at a time and adopt Joyce's (1992) approach to staff development that encompasses demonstration, practice, observation and feedback. Across all the projects, an instructional framework provides the teaching strategies and approaches required to secure improved student outcomes.

7. *Investing in teaching*. Teacher development is a major component of all successful school improvement programmes. Research has shown that professional development is usually most effective when it is not delivered by extraneous experts in off-site locations, but when it is embedded in the school and when it is the focus of collaborative discussion and action (Little 1993). In many of the programmes, staff development is school-based and classroom focused. The main thrust of the work with teachers in each of the projects is to equip them to manage classroom change, development and improvement.
8. *Building professional communities*. In several projects (e.g. Accelerated Schools, IQEA), teachers are actively encouraged to build their own professional communities both within and outside the school. Emphasis is placed upon teacher collaboration and networking. The net result of this activity is not only the sharing of good practice, but the establishment of professional development communities within the school that can sustain and maintain development.
9. *Enquiry led*. The importance of enquiry and reflection within the process of school improvement has long been established. Levine and Lezotte (1990) noted that a 'commitment to inquiry' was a consistent feature of highly effective schools. The analysis and application of research findings by teachers as part of their routine professional activity has been shown to have had a positive effect on the quality of teaching and learning (Hopkins *et al.* 1997; Harris and Hopkins 1999). There is evidence from highly successful school improvement projects that providing teachers with the opportunity to enquire into their practice has resulted in changed attitudes, beliefs and behaviours. Moreover, that these changes in attitudes, beliefs and behaviours have directly affected their classroom teaching and resulted in improved learning outcomes for students.

All successful school improvement involves change and requires schools to manage and implement the change process. To ensure that change is fully implemented, schools have to put in place the necessary systems, processes and structures. It is clear that the most effective school improvement programmes assist schools to 'build the capacity' for implementing change and improvement. In other words, through a combination of pressure and support they are able to assist schools in generating both the *readiness to change* and the *internal capacity* to manage the change process.

External agency. Evaluative evidence illustrates that school improvement cannot progress without the influence of external and internal 'agency'. Earl and Lee (1998) describe successful school improvement as a chain reaction of 'urgency, energy, agency and more energy'. Their work suggests that building the capacity for school improvement requires both internal and external forces for change and development. As noted earlier in this book and most recently by Lieberman and Miller (2004), there is a vast range of research describing the existence, development and contribution of teacher leadership to school development, change and improvement. Indeed, teacher leadership is generally thought to be a pre-condition for school improvement (Smylie 1995; Wasley 1991). A great deal of this work has focused upon how teachers' roles might be redefined to include responsibilities for decision making and involvement in democratic processes of change. Both Fullan (2001) and Lambert (2003) replace this rather narrow vision of teacher leadership with a broader notion in which the leadership of teachers is grounded in what Lambert (2003) calls 'relationships, community learning and purpose' (p.14). Essentially, teacher leadership is more than individual enterprise – it is conceived of as being the collective driving force for change.

Change agentry. It is clear from this book and elsewhere (e.g. Frost and Durrant, 2002; Lieberman and Miller 2004) that teacher leadership is essentially a form of 'change agentry'. The term 'agentry' is well known within the school improvement literature and means those individuals or groups of individuals who are charged with the responsibility for leading school-level change. Teacher leaders who operate as facilitators, coordinators or mentors occupy a position that is critical to the successful implementation of school improvement (Datnow *et al.* 2003). The following overview of one highly successful school improvement project in England provides some insight into how teachers act as change agents and contribute to school improvement.

Teacher leadership and school improvement in action

One of the most successful school improvement projects in the UK is Improving the Quality of Education for All (IQEA). This school improvement project is chiefly concerned with change agentry and building collaborative cultures in schools. IQEA is premised on the view that 'without an equal focus on the development capacity, or internal conditions of the school, innovative work quickly becomes marginalised' (Hopkins *et al.* 1997: 3). Essentially, IQEA is a model of school change that is premised upon facilitating cultural change within schools primarily through teacher leadership. It is not prescriptive in terms of what schools actually do, but does define the parameters for development. It provides an overarching model for school improvement which schools subsequently adapt for their own purposes and fit to their particular needs and context. IQEA is research driven and encourages schools not only to engage in their own internal enquiry, but also to utilize the external research base on effective teaching and learning.

IQEA began in 1991 with nine schools in East Anglia, North London and Yorkshire. By 2003 it had grown to involve over fifty schools in twelve local education authorities around the country and has been trialled in locations as diverse as Hong Kong and Scandinavia. IQEA has two core aims. The first relates to developing a model of school development underpinned by empirical evidence. The second is to improve schools by developing and spreading good practice among teachers. Hopkins *et al.* (1994) state the overall aim is to: 'produce and evaluate a model for school development and a programme of support that strengthen a school's ability to provide high-quality education for all pupils by building on existing good practice' (p. 7). They go on to describe IQEA as 'A collaborative enterprise designed to strengthen their [school leaders'] ability to manage change, to enhance the work of teachers, and ultimately to improve the outcomes, however, broadly defined, of students' (pp. 100–1).

As Stoll and Fink (1996) note, for a school to be involved with the programme, all staff must agree that the school will be involved and at least 40 per cent must receive release time to conduct IQEA activity. Each school can select its own priorities for development, and its own methods for achieving these priorities, thus increasing ownership of the change process (Fullan 1991). The school must also agree to participate in the evaluation of the programme and to share the project findings. In practice, the programme works at three levels. First, at the individual classroom level, where teachers (and in some cases students) work on developing their practices through classroom-based research, including action enquiry (see Hopkins, 2001). Second, at the whole-school level, where a cross-hierarchical group of teacher leaders is formed (cadre or school improvement group) to drive and coordinate the programme. Third, individual schools do not work in isolation. All schools within the project form part of a network which varies in size from those containing only a few schools to the involvement of all secondary schools. The aim of this networking is to generate teacher leadership within and between schools and to generate what Hargreaves (2004: 4) calls 'successful innovation through networking'.

Development work at the schools is underpinned by support from external (usually but not exclusively university-based) consultants. The role of this external support is to provide critical friendship to the school. This external perspective is viewed as an important part of the process, providing challenge and support within a trusting relationship independent of local educational authorities or central government agencies. The external consultant is also a resource that the schools can draw upon. They may be expected to provide up-to-date knowledge of developments in the fields of effectiveness and improvement.

Reynolds *et al.* (1996: 146) suggest that the most important finding from IQEA is that school improvement works best when a clear and practical focus for development is linked to simultaneous work on the internal conditions within the school. These efforts exhibit three elements:

- providing internal and external support structures for change;
- creating the internal conditions that will sustain and manage change in schools;
- focusing on teacher leadership as the agent of change.

Within the project, teachers are the mobilizing force behind development, while the senior management team might provide the overall direction; there is a high degree of autonomy and self-direction among the school improvement or cadre groups. The stages of teacher leadership characterized by the project are threefold. These are: the initiation or 'getting started' stage; the keeping up momentum stage; and the monitoring and evaluating progress and success stage. This cycle is very similar to that experienced as part of the action research process, which is driven by the need for teachers to solve practical, real-world problems. In action research and IQEA, research and enquiry are concerned with practical issues that arise naturally as part of professional activity. Action enquiry is participatory in design, as it involves the active participation of the researcher and those participating in the research. There are many different approaches to action enquiry but the typical stages are as follows:

- identification of a problem or concern;
- collection of information;
- analysis of information;
- decisions about action;

- take action;
- evaluate impact of action.

The GTC/NUT study showed that teacher leaders are engaged in many aspects of action enquiry and reflection. Consistent with the findings from research on externally developed reforms, the extent of teacher involvement and ownership is an important prerequisite of success. Teacher leaders can be both facilitators and obstacles to change. In the case study schools in the GTC/NUT study, there were clear examples of where development was accompanied by genuine as well as contrived forms of collegiality. While a true collaborative culture among teachers can be a powerful force for school improvement (Lieberman 1988), a contrived collegiality means that teachers may be coerced to work together in ways that are less than optimum for development. As Hargreaves (1994) notes, collaboration among teachers who have these characteristics (of contrived collegiality) will not generally lead to meaningful change. In schools like school C, where the professional culture did not support collaboration, the drive for distributed leadership resulted in factionalism and, in some cases, mistrust among teachers.

Connected to the extent of collaboration among teachers was the extent to which teacher learning and empowerment were present. In school A, the empowerment derived from teachers having a greater role in school decision making. In other schools it came from the use of a new teaching model that allowed teachers to communicate more freely and openly. At the same time there were teachers who felt disempowered by the drive towards distributed leadership and, indeed, by the leadership in their schools. It was clear that in one or two cases opportunities occurred for some teachers and not for others. Where teachers were singled out for leadership roles and given associated responsibility and reward, it did not generate participation by other teachers in leadership activity.

It was also clear from the GTC/NUT project that where teacher leadership was working successfully, enhanced professional development opportunities were available. Like teacher empowerment, the presence of professional development opportunities was a key indicator of mutual teacher learning and leading. While the particular professional development experiences varied from school to school, it was evident that opportunities for teachers to work and learn together in a formal way (i.e. through networked learning communities, IQEA, education action zones) had a significant impact on the quality of innovative work within and between schools. It was also clear that the relationship between the head and teachers was a critical component of successful teacher leadership. The study showed that the range of actions taken by headteachers to generate teacher leadership influenced the subsequent activities and relationships of teachers, making them more or less effective in driving change forward. There was a wide variation in the levels of teacher empowerment and teacher learning that took place as a direct result of the way in which the head managed the process.

Towards a new professionalism?

If, as this book suggests, there is a powerful relationship between teacher leadership and school improvement, there are important ramifications for teaching as a profession and for teacher professionalism *per se*. Lieberman and Miller (2004) suggest that the demands of teaching in a new century coupled with the drift towards teachers as leaders requires a new set of propositions about teaching which represent major shifts in perspective and practice. These shifts include:

- *From individualism to professional community*. When teachers view their work as taking place both within and beyond their own classrooms, they participate in an authentic learning community. They build capacity for joint work and develop norms of collegiality, openness, trust, experimentation, risk taking and feedback. Teaching becomes public and more open to critique and improvement; it promotes an expanded view of professional responsibility and accountability – a move from concerns about my students in my classroom to our students in our school.
- *From teaching at the centre to learning at the centre*. When teachers shift their attention from the act of teaching to the process of learning, they corroborate for each other that 'one size fits few'. By looking collaboratively at student work and designing curriculum, assessments and instructional strategies together, they gain the collective knowledge, confidence and power to co-construct alternatives to standardized approaches and measures.
- *From technical and managed work to inquiry and leadership*. When teachers cast off the mantle of technical and managed worker and assume new roles as researchers, meaning makers, scholars and inventors, they expand the vision of who they are and what they do. They come to view themselves, and are viewed by others, as intellectuals engaged in inquiry about teaching and learning. Central to this expanded vision is the idea of teachers as leaders, educators who can make a difference in schools and schooling now and in the future (Lieberman and Miller 2004).

The implication of this set of propositions is a radically different way of viewing teachers and teaching. It implies new roles and responsibilities as teachers become the central innovators and instigators of change.

As Hargreaves (2004) has outlined 'for teachers most innovation is the creation of new professional knowledge about their work' (p.6). He makes the distinction between radical innovation, where there is discontinuity between the new practice and the one it displaces, and incremental innovation, where there is a gradual evolution of practice into something better. The nature of the innovation will largely be the decision of the teachers embarking on the transformation or innovation. The central point here is that innovation, development and change are no longer defined by those outside schools but predominantly guided, shaped and delivered by teachers within and across schools.

Consequently, a new professionalism is emerging that places teachers, for the first time, at the epicentre of change and development. It suggests that teachers will be:

- Stewards of a new, invigorated profession characterized by creativity, innovation and a desire to share best practice.
- Advocates for new forms of accountability and assessment that encompass professional judgement and give credence to self-evaluation.
- Instigators of new ways of relating, working and engaging with each other as a profession.
- Leaders of learning, where their efforts build professional learning communities for themselves and their students (adapted from Lieberman and Miller 2004).

It is clear that in the last three decades or so there has been a dramatic shift away from teacher professionalism towards teacher accountability. Many have argued that teaching has been de-professionalized and reduced to the lowest common denominator of standards, testing and inspection. However, as the successive failures of top-down reforms and accountability systems to improve educational systems become more apparent, there is an urgent need for alternative solutions to improving schools. This book has highlighted the potential of teacher leadership as a powerful lever for change and development. It has shown that where teachers work together in meaningful partnerships, much can be achieved for the benefit of schools and the young people who learn there. The inadequacies of standards-based reform mean that education is at last reclaimable for those who have been disenfranchised for several decades. There is no better time for teachers to be leaders, to initiate, innovate and drive development work. If we are serious about building learning communities or networks, this cannot be done without relocating leadership closer to the classroom. The professional challenges may be great but the professional rewards will be even greater if we simply allow, empower and enable teachers to lead and to make the difference denied to them for so long.

References

Argyris, C. and Schön, D. (1974) *Theory in Practice: Increasing Professional Effectiveness*. San Francisco, CA: Jossey-Bass.

Ash, R.C. and Persall, J.M. (2000) The principal as chief learning officer: developing teacher leaders, *NASSP Bulletin*, 84(616): 15–22.

Askew, M., Rhodes, V., Brown, M., William, D. and Johnson, D. (1998) *Effective Teachers of Numeracy*. Report of a Study Conducted for the Teacher Training Agency. London: King's College London, School of Education.

Barth, R. (1990) *Improving Schools From Within: Teachers, Parents and Principals Can Make a Difference*. San Francisco, CA: Jossey-Bass.

Barth, R. (1999) *The Teacher Leader*. Providence, RI: The Rhode Island Foundation.

Barth, R. (2000) Building a community of learners, *Principal*, 79(4): 68–9.

Bascia, N. (1997) Invisible leadership: teachers' union activity in schools, *Alberta Journal of Educational Research*, 43(2–3): 69–85.

Bell, L., Bolam, R. and Cubillo, L. (2003) *A Systematic Review of the Impact of School Headteachers and Principals on Student Outcomes*. EPPI Centre Review. London: Institute of Education.

Bennett, N., Harvey, J.A., Wise, C. and Woods, P.A. (2003) *Distributed Leadership: A Desk Study* (available at: www.ncsl.org.uk/literaturereviews).

Berends, M., Bodilly, S. and Kirby, S. (2002) *Facing the Challenges of Whole School Reform: New American Schools after a Decade*. Santa Monica, CA: Rand.

Biott, C. (1991) *Semi-Detached Teachers: Building Support and Advisory Relationships in Classrooms*. London: Falmer Press.

Blase, J. and Anderson, G. (1995) *The Micro-Politics of Educational Leadership: From Control to Empowerment*. London: Cassell.

Boles, K. (1992) School restructuring by teachers: a study of the teaching project at the Edward Devotion School. Paper presented at the Annual Meeting of the American Educational Research Association, San Francisco, CA, April.

Boles, K. and Troen, V. (1994) Teacher leadership in a Professional Development School. Paper presented at the Annual Meeting of the American Educational Research Association, New Orleans, LA, April.

Bottery, M. (2002) Professional learning communities in a climate of mistrust. Paper presented at *ESRC Seminar*, University of Warwick, November.

Boyd, V. (1992) *School Context: Bridge or Barrier to Change?* Austin, TX: Southwest Educational Development Laboratory.

Brophy, J.E. and Good, T.L. (1988) Teacher behaviour and student achievement, in M.C. Wittrock (ed.) *Handbook of Research on Teaching*. New York: Macmillan.

Bryk, A. and Schneider, B. (2003) *Trust in Schools*. New York: Russell Sage Foundation.

Buckner, K.C. and McDowell, J. (2000) Developing teacher leaders: providing encouragement, opportunities and support, *NASSP Bulletin*, 84(616): 35–41.

Bush, T. and Glover, D. (2003) *School Leadership: Concepts and Evidence* (available at: www.ncsl.org.uk/literaturereviews).

Caine, G. and Caine, R.N. (2000) The learning community as a foundation for developing teacher leaders, *NASSP Bulletin*, 84: 7–14.

Campbell, R.J. and Neill, S.R.StJ. (1994) *Primary Teachers at Work*. London: Routledge.

Campbell, R.J., Kyriakides, L., Muijs, D. and Robinson, W. (2003) Differential teacher effectiveness: towards a model for research and teacher appraisal, *Oxford Review of Education*, 29(3): 347–62.

Childs-Bowen, D., Moller, G. and Scrivner, J. (2000) Principals: leaders of leaders, *NASSP Bulletin*, 84(6): 27–34.

Clemson-Ingram, R. and Fessler, R. (1997) Innovative programs for teacher leadership, *Action in Teacher Education*, 19(3): 95–106.

Crowther, F., Kaagan, S., Ferguson, M. and Hann, L. (2002) *Developing Teacher Leaders: How Teacher Leadership Enhances School Success*. Thousand Oaks, CA: Corwin Press.

Darling-Hammond, L. (1990) Teacher professionalism: why and how?, in A. Lieberman (ed.) *Schools as Collaborative Cultures: Creating the Future Now*. London: Falmer Press.

Darling-Hammond, L. (1996) The quiet revolution: rethinking teacher development, *Educational Leadership*, 53(6): 4–10.

Datnow, A., Hubbard, L. and Mehan, H. (2003) *Extending Educational Reform*. London: Falmer Press.

Davidson, B. and Taylor D. (1999) Examining principal succession and teacher leadership in school restructuring. Paper presented at the Annual Meeting of the American Educational Research Association, Montreal, Quebec, April.

Day, C., Harris, A., Hadfield, M., Tolley, H. and Beresford, J. (2000) *Leading Schools in Times of Change*. Buckingham: Open University Press.

Desimone, L. (2000) *Making Comprehensive School Reform Work*. New York: ERIC Clearinghouse on Urban Education.

Dickerson, C. (1992) The lead teacher model: a restructured school. Paper presented at the Annual Meeting of the North Carolina Association of Research in Education, Chapel Hill, NC.

Earl, L. and Lee, L. (1998) *Evaluation of Manitoba School Improvement Project*. Final Report, University of Manitoba and University of Toronto.

Eastwood, K. and Louis, K. (1992) Restructuring that lasts: managing the performance dip, *Journal of School Leadership*, 2(2): 213–24.

Elmore, R. (2000) *Building a New Structure for School Leadership*. Washington, DC: The Albert Shanker Institute.

Elmore, R. and Sykes, G. (1992) Curriculum policy, in P. Jacson (ed.) *Handbook of Research in Curriculum*. New York: Macmillan.

Engeström, Y. (1999) Activity theory and individual and social transformation, in Y. Engestrom, R. Mietten and R.-L. Punamäki (eds) *Perspectives on Activity Theory*. Cambridge: Cambridge University Press.

Evans, L. (1998) *Teachers' Motivation*. London: Continuum Press.

Fawcett, G. (1996) Moving another big desk, *Journal of Staff Development*, 17(1): 34–6.

Frost, D. and Durrant, J. (2002) *Teacher-Led Development Work: Guidance and Support*. London: David Fulton.

Fullan, M. (1991) *The New Meaning of Educational Change*. London: Cassell.

Fullan, M. (1993) *Change Forces: Probing the Depths of Educational Reform*. London: Falmer Press.

Fullan, M. (1999) *Change Forces: The Sequel*. Buckingham: Open University Press.

Fullan, M. (2001) *Leading in a Culture of Change*. San Francisco, CA: Jossey-Bass.

Gehrke, N. (1991) *Developing Teachers' Leadership Skills*. ERIC Digest ED330691.

Gibb, C.A. (1954) Leadership, in G. Lindzey (ed.) *Handbook of Social Psychology* (Vol. 2). Reading, MA: Addison-Wesley.

Giddens, A. (1984) *The Constitution of Society*. Cambridge: Polity Press.

Glickman, C., Gordon, S. and Ross-Gordon, J. (2001) *Supervision and Instructional Leadership: A Developmental Approach*. Boston, MA: Allyn & Bacon.

Gold, A., Evans, J., Early, P., Halpin, D. and Collabone, P. (2002) Principled principals. Value driven leadership: evidence from ten case studies. Paper presented at the Annual Meeting of the American Educational Research Association, New Orleans, LA, April.

Goleman, D. (2002) *The New Leaders: Transforming the Art of Leadership into the Science of Results*. London: Little, Brown & Co.

Greenleaf, R.K. (1996) *On Becoming a Servant Leader*. San Francisco, CA: Jossey-Bass.

Griffin, G.A. (1995) Influences of shared decision making on school and classroom activity: conversations with five teachers, *Elementary School Journal*, 96(1): 29–45.

Gronn, P. (2000) Distributed properties: a new architecture for leadership, *Educational Management and Administration*, 28(3): 317–83.

Gronn, P. (2003) *The New Work of Educational Leaders: Changing Leadership Practice in the Era of School Reform*. London: Paul Chapman.

Hackney, C.E. and Henderson, J.G. (1999) Educating school leaders for inquiry-based democratic learning communities, *Educational Horizons*, 77(2): 67–73.

Hallinger, P. and Heck, R.H. (1996a) The principal's role in school effectiveness: an assessment of methodological progress, 1980–1995, in K. Leithwood, J. Chapman, D. Corsan, P. Hallinger and A. Hart (eds.) *International Handbook of*

Educational Leadership and Administration (Vol. 2). Dordrecht, The Netherlands: Kluwer Academic.

Hallinger, P. and Heck, R. (1996b) The principal's role in school effectiveness: a critical review of empirical research 1980–1995, *Educational Administration Quarterly*, 32(1): 5–24.

Hargreaves, A. (1991) Restructuring restructuring: postmodernity and the prospects for educational change. Paper presented at the Annual Meeting of the American Educational Research Association, Chicago, IL, April.

Hargreaves, A. (1994) *Changing Teachers: Changing Times.* London: Cassell.

Hargreaves, A. (2002) Professional learning communities and performance training cults: the emerging apartheid of school improvement, in A. Harris, D. Hopkins, A. Hargreaves *et al., Effective Leadership for School Improvement.* London: Routledge.

Hargreaves, A. (2004) *Teaching in the Knowledge Society.* New York: Teachers College Press.

Harris, A. (1999) *Teaching and Learning in the Effective School.* London: Arena Press.

Harris, A. (2000a) Successful school improvement in the United Kingdom and Canada, *Canadian Journal of Education, Administration and Policy*, 15: 1–8.

Harris, A. (2000b) What works in school improvement? Lessons from the field and future directions, *Educational Research*, 42(1): 1–11.

Harris, A. (2000c) Effective leadership and departmental improvement, *Westminster Studies in Education*, 23: 81–90.

Harris, A. (2001) Building the capacity for school improvement, *School Leadership and Management*, 21(3): 261–70.

Harris, A. (2002a) *School Improvement: What's in it for Schools?* London: Falmer Press.

Harris, A. (2002b) Distributed leadership: leading or misleading? Keynote address to the Annual Conference of BELMAS, Aston University, Birmingham, October.

Harris, A. (2003) Teacher leadership: a new orthodoxy, in B. Davies and J. West Burnham (eds) *The Handbook of Educational Leadership and Management.* London: Pearson Press.

Harris, A. and Chapman, C. (2002) *Effective Leadership in Schools Facing Challenging Circumstances.* Final Report. Nottingham: National College for School Leadership.

Harris, A. and Hopkins, D. (1999) Teaching and learning and the challenge of educational reform, *School Effectiveness and School Improvement: An International Journal of Research Policy and Practice*, 10(1): 257–67.

Harris, A. and Lambert, L. (2003) *Building Leadership Capacity for School Improvement.* Buckingham: Open University Press.

Harris, A. and Muijs, D. (2003) *Teacher Leadership: A Review of the Literature* (available at: GTC and NUT websites).

Hart, A.W. (1995) Reconceiving school leadership: emergent views, *Elementary School Journal*, 96(1): 9–28.

Helm, C. (1989) Cultural and symbolic leadership in Catholic elementary schools: an ethnographic study. Unpublished doctoral dissertation, Catholic University of America, Washington, DC.

Holden, G. (2002) Towards a learning community: the role of teacher-led development in school improvement. Paper presented at the CELSI British Council Leadership in Learning Conference, London.

Hopkins, D. (2001) *School Improvement for Real*. London: Falmer Press.

Hopkins, D. and Harris, A. (2000) Differential strategies for school development, in D. Van Veen and C. Day (eds) *Professional Development and School Improvement: Strategies for Growth*. Mahwah, NJ: Erlbaum.

Hopkins, D. and Jackson, D. (2003) Building the capacity for leading and learning, in A. Harris, D. Hopkins, A. Hargreaves *et al.*, *Effective Leadership for School Improvement*. London: Routledge.

Hopkins, D., Ainscow, M. and West, M. (1994) *School Improvement in an Era of Change*. London: Cassell.

Hopkins, D., Harris, A. and Jackson, D. (1997) Understanding the school's capacity for development: growth states and strategies, *School Leadership and Management*, 17(3): 401–11.

Hord, S.M. and Huling-Austin, L. (1986) Effective curriculum implementation: some promising new insights, *Elementary School Journal*, 87(1): 97–115.

Jackson, D. (2000) The school improvement journey: perspectives on leadership, *School Leadership and Management*, 20(1): 61–79.

Joyce, B. (1992) Cooperative learning and staff development: teaching the method with the method, *Cooperative Learning*, 12(2): 10–13.

Katzenmeyer, M. and Moller, G. (2001) *Awakening the Sleeping Giant: Helping Teachers Develop as Leaders*. Thousand Oaks, CA: Corwin Press.

Kets de Vries, M.F.R. (1990) The organizational fool: balancing a leader's hubis, *Human Relations*, 43(8) 751–70.

King, M.B. (1996) Participatory decision making, in M.B. King (ed.) *Restructuring for Authentic Student Achievement: The Impact of Culture and Structure in 24 Schools*. San Francisco, CA: Jossey-Bass.

Klette, K. (2000) Working-time blues: how Norwegian teachers experience restructuring in education, in C. Day, A. Fernandez, T.E. Hauge and J. Moller (eds) *The Life and Work of Teachers: International Perspectives in Changing Times*. London: Falmer Press.

Krisko, M.E. (2001) Teacher leadership: a profile to identify the potential. Paper presented at the Biennial Convocation of Kappa Delta Phi, Orlando, FL, November.

Lambert, L. (1998) *Building Leadership Capacity in Schools*. Alexandria, VA: Association for Supervision and Curriculum Development.

Lambert, L. (2003) *Leadership Capacity for Lasting School Improvement*. Alexandria, VA: Association for Supervision and Curriculum Development.

LeBlanc, P.R. and Skelton, M.M. (1997) Teacher leadership: the needs of teachers, *Action in Teacher Education*, 19(3): 32–48.

Leithwood, K. and Jantzi, D. (1990) Transformational leadership: how principals can help reform school cultures, *School Effectiveness and School Improvement: An International Journal of Research, Policy and Practice*, 1(4): 249–80.

Leithwood, K. and Jantzi, D. (2000) The effects of transformational leadership on organisational conditions and student engagement, *Journal of Educational Administration*, 38(2): 112–29.

Leithwood, K. and Reil, C. (2003) *What We Know About Successful School Leadership*. Brief prepared for the Task Force on Developing Research in Educational Leadership, Division A, American Educational Research Association. Philadelphia, PA: Temple University

Leithwood, K., Jantzi, D. and Steinback, R. (1999) *Changing Leadership for Changing Times*. Buckingham: Open University Press.

Leithwood, K., Jantzi, D., Earl, L. *et al.* (2004) Leadership for large scale reform: the case of England's National Literacy and Numeracy Strategy, School Leadership and Management, 24(1): 27–41.

Lemlech, J.K. and Hertzog, H. (1998) Preparing teachers for leadership roles. Paper presented at the Annual Meeting of the American Educational Research Association, San Diego, CA, April.

Levine, D. and Lezotte, L. (1990) *Unusually Effective Schools: A Review of Research and Practice*. Madison, WI: National Centre for Effective Schools Research and Development.

Lieberman, A. (1988) Teachers and principals: turf, tension and new tasks, *Phi Delta Kappa*, 69: 648–53.

Lieberman, A. and Miller, L. (2004) *Teacher Leadership*. San Francisco, CA: Jossey-Bass.

Lieberman, A., Saxl, E.R. and Miles, M.B. (2000) Teacher leadership: ideology and practice, in *The Jossey-Bass Reader on Educational Leadership*. San Francisco, CA: Jossey-Bass.

Little, J.W. (1990) The persistence of privacy: autonomy and initiative in teachers' professional relations, *Teacher College Record*, 91: 55–6.

Little, J.W. (1993) Teachers' professional development in a climate of educational reform, *Educational Evaluation and Policy Analysis*, 15(2): 129–51.

Little, J.W. (1995) Contested ground: the basis of teacher leadership in two restructuring high schools, *Elementary School Journal*, 96(1): 47–63.

Little, J.W. (2000) Assessing the prospects for teacher leadership, in *The Jossey-Bass Reader on Educational Leadership*. San Francisco, CA: Jossey-Bass.

Little, J.W. (2002) Locating learning in teachers' communities of practice: opening up problems of analysis in records of everyday work, *Teaching and Teacher Education*, 18(8): 917–46.

Louis, K.S. and Kruse, S. (1995) *Professionalism and the Community: Perspectives on Reforming Urban Schools*. Thousand Oaks, CA: Corwin Press.

Louis, K. and Marks, H. (1996) Teachers' professional community in restructuring schools, *American Educational Research Journal*, 33(4): 757–89.

Louis, K.S. and Miles, M.B. (1990) *Improving the Urban High School: What Works and Why*. New York: Teachers College Press.

MacBeath, J. (ed.) (1998) *Effective School Leadership: Responding to Change*. London: Paul Chapman.

Magee, M. (1999) Curse of the trophy, *Journal of Staff Development*, 20(4): 23–6.

McLaughlin, M.W. and Talbert, J.E. (1993) *Contexts that Matter for Teaching and Learning*. Stanford, CA: Center for Research on the Context of Secondary School Teaching, Stanford University.

McMahon, A., Thomas, S., Smith, M. *et al.* (2003) Effective professional learning communities. Paper presented to the British Educational Research Association Conference, Edinburgh, September.

Midgley, C. and Wood, S. (1993) Beyond site-based management: empowering teachers to reform schools, *Phi Delta Kappa*, 75(3): 245–52.

Mitchell, C. and Sackney, L. (2001) *Profound Improvement: Building Capacity for a Learning Community*. Lisse: Swets & Zeitlinger.

Morrissey, M. (2000) Professional learning communities: an ongoing exploration. Unpublished paper, Southwest Educational Development Laboratory, Austin, TX.

Mortimore, P., Sammons, P., Stoll, L., Lewis, D. and Ecob, R. (1988) *School Matters*. Wells, UK: Open Books.

Muijs, D. and Harris, A. (2003) Teacher leadership: improvement through empowerment, *Educational Management and Administration*, 31(4): 437–49.

Muijs, D. and Reynolds, D. (2000) School effectiveness and teacher effectiveness: some preliminary findings from the evaluation of the Mathematics Enhancement Programme, *School Effectiveness and School Improvement: An International Journal of Research, Policy and Practice*, 11(3): 247–63.

Muijs, D. and Reynolds, D. (2001) *Effective Teaching: Evidence and Practice*. London: Paul Chapman.

Muijs, D. and Reynolds, D. (2002) Teacher beliefs and behaviors: what matters, *Journal of Classroom Interaction*, 37(2): 3–15.

Muijs, D. and Reynolds, D. (2003) Student background and teacher effects on achievement and attainment in mathematics, *Educational Research and Evaluation*, 9(1): 21–35.

Murphy, J. (2000) The effects of the educational reform movement on departments of educational leadership, *Educational Evaluation and Policy Analysis*, 13(1): 49–65.

Nemerowicz, G. and Rosi, E. (1997) *Education for Leadership and Social Responsibility*. New York: Praeger.

Newmann, F.M., King, M.B. and Youngs, P. (2000) Professional development that addresses school capacity: lessons from urban elementary schools, *American Journal of Education*, 108(4): 259–99.

O'Connor, K. and Boles, K. (1992) Assessing the needs of teacher leaders in Massachusetts. Paper presented at the Annual Meeting of the American Educational Research Association, San Francisco, CA, April.

Ogawa, R.T. and Bossert, S.T. (1995) Leadership as an organizational quality, *Educational Administration Quarterly*, 31(2): 224–43.

Ovando, M. (1994) Effects of teachers' leadership on their teaching practices. Paper presented at the Annual Conference of the University Council of Educational Administration, Philadelphia, PA, October.

Ovando, M. (1996) Teacher leadership: opportunities and challenges, *Planning and Change*, 27(1/2): 30–44.

Pechman, E. and King, J. (1993) *Obstacles to Restructuring: Experiences of Six Middle-Grades Schools*. New York: Teachers College Press.

Pellicer, L.O. and Anderson, L.W. (1995) *A Handbook for Teacher Leaders*. Thousand Oaks, CA: Corwin Press.

Peterson, K.D., Murphy, J. and Hallinger, P. (1987) Superintendents' perceptions of

the control and coordination of the technical core in effective school districts, *Educational Administration Quarterly*, 23(1): 79–95.
Reynolds, D., Sammons, P., Stoll, L., Barber, M. and Hillman, J. (1996) School effectiveness and school improvement in the United Kingdom, *School Effectiveness and School Improvement: An International Journal of Research, Policy and Practice*, 7(2): 133–58.
Rosenholz, S. (1989) *Teachers' Workplace: The Social Organization of Schools*. New York: Teachers College Press.
Sackney, L., Walker, K. and Hajal, V. (1998) Principal and teacher perspectives on school improvement, *Journal of Educational Management*, 1(1): 45–63.
Sammons, P., Thomas, S. and Mortimore, P. (1997) *Forging Links: Effective Schools and Effective Departments*. London: Paul Chapman.
Schaffer, E.C., Muijs, R.D., Kitson, C. and Reynolds, D. (1998) *Mathematics Enhancement Classroom Observation Record*. Newcastle upon Tyne: Educational Effectiveness and Improvement Centre.
Scheerens, J. (1992) *Effective Schooling: Research, Theory and Practice*. London: Cassell.
Seashore-Louis, K.S. and Kruse, S. (1996) Putting teachers at the centre of reform: learning schools and professional communities, *Bulletin*, May, pp. 10–21.
Senge, P. (1990) *The Fifth Discipline: The Art and Practice of the Learning Organisation*. New York: Doubleday.
Sergiovanni, T.J. (1994) *Building Community in Schools*. San Francisco, CA: Jossey-Bass.
Sergiovanni, T.J. (1996) *Leadership for the Schoolhouse*. San Francisco, CA: Jossey-Bass.
Sergiovanni, T. (2000) *The Lifeworld of Leadership*. London: Jossey-Bass.
Sherrill, J.A. (1999) Preparing teachers for leadership roles, *Theory into Practice*, 38: 56–67.
Sickler, J.L. (1988) Teachers in charge: empowering the professionals, *Phi Delta Kappa*, 69(5): 354–6.
Silins, H. and Mulford, B. (2002) Leadership and school results, in K. Leithwood and P. Hallinger (eds) *Second International Handbook of Educational Leadership and Administration*. Norwell, MA: Kluwer Academic.
Smylie, M.A. (1995) New perspectives on teacher leadership, *Elementary School Journal*, 96(1): 3–7.
Snell, J. and Swanson, J. (2000) The essential knowledge and skills of teacher leaders: a search for a conceptual framework. Paper presented at the Annual Meeting of the American Educational Research Association, New Orleans, LA, April.
Snyder, K.J., Acker-Hocevar, M. and Snyder, K.M. (1996) Principals speak out on changing school work cultures, *Journal of Staff Development*, 17(1): 14–19.
Spillane, J.P., Halverson, R. and Diamond, J.B. (2001a) Investigating school leadership practice: a distributed perspective, *Educational Researcher*, 30(3): 23–8.
Spillane, J., Halverson, R. and Diamond, J. (2001b) *Towards a Theory of Leadership Practice: A Distributed Perspective*. Institute for Policy Research Working Article, Northwestern University.

Stoll, L. and Fink, D. (1996) *Changing Our Schools: Linking School Effectiveness and School Improvement*. Buckingham: Open University Press.
Stoll, L., Bolam, R., McMahon, A. *et al.* (2003) Creating and sustaining effective learning communities. Paper presented to the International Congress of School Effectiveness and School Improvement, Sydney, NSW, January.
Taylor, D.L. and Bogotch, I.E. (1994) School-level effects of teachers' participation in decision making, *Educational Evaluation and Policy Analysis*, 16(3): 302–19.
Teacher Training Agency (1998) *Subject Leader Standards*. London: TTA.
Teddlie, C. and Reynolds, D. (2000) *The International Handbook of School Effectiveness Research*. London: Falmer Press.
Tedesco, J.C. (1997) What education for what citizenship?, *Educational Innovation*, 90(1): 45–59.
Toole, J.C. (2001) *Mental Models, Professional Learning Communities and the Deep Structure of School Change: Case Studies of Service Learning*. Minneapolis, MN: University of Minnesota Press.
Toole, J.C. and Seashore-Louis, K.S. (2002) *The Role of Professional Learning Communities in International Education* (available at: education.umn.edu/ CAREI/Papers/ JULYFINAL. pdf).
Troen, V. and Boles, K. (1992) Leadership from the classroom: women teachers as the key to school reform. Paper presented at the Annual Meeting of the American Educational Research Association, San Francisco, CA, April.
Vasquez-Levy, D. and Timmerman, M.A. (2000) Beyond the classroom: connecting and empowering teachers as leaders, *Teaching and Change*, 7(4): 363–71.
Wagstaff, L. and Reyes, P. (1993) *School-Based Site Management*. Austin, TX: University of Texas at Austin.
Wallace, M. (2002) Modeling distributed leadership and management effectiveness: primary school senior management teams in England and Wales, *School Effectiveness and School Improvement: An International Journal on Research, Policy and Practice*, 13(2): 163–86.
Wasley, P.A. (1991) From quarterback to coach, from actor to director, *Educational Leadership*, 48(8): 35–40.
Watts, G.D. and Castle, S. (1993) The time dilemma in school restructuring, *Phi Delta Kappa*, 75(3): 306–10.
Weiss, C.H. and Cambone, J. (1994) Principals, shared decision making, and school reform, *Educational Evaluation and Policy Analysis*, 16(3): 287–301.
Wenger, E. (1998) *Communities of Practice: Learning, Meaning and Identity*. Cambridge: Cambridge University Press.
Wenger, E., McDermott, R. and Snyder, W. (2002) *Cultivating Communities of Practice: A Guide to Managing Knowledge*. Storrs, CT: Harvard University Press.
West, M., Jackson, D., Harris, A. and Hopkins, D. (2000) Leadership for school improvement, in K. Riley and K. Seashore-Louis (eds) *Leadership for Change*. London: Routledge/Falmer.
Wheatley, M. (2000) Good-bye command and control, in *The Jossey-Bass Reader on Educational Leadership*. San Francisco, CA: Jossey-Bass.
Wong, K. (1996) *Prospects. Special Analyses*. Final Reports. Chicago, IL: US Department of Education.

Woods, P.A. (2004) Democratic leadership: drawing distinctions with distributed leadership, *International Journal of Leadership in Education*, 7(1): 3–26.
Zinn, L.F. (1997) Supports and barriers to teacher leadership: reports on teacher leaders: Paper presented at the Annual Meeting of the American Educational Research Association, Chicago, IL, April.

Index

LEADERSHIP, GENDER AND CULTURE IN EDUCATION
Male and female perspectives

John Collard and Cecilia Reynolds (eds)

This edited collection contains chapters by some of the world's leading scholars on gender and educational leadership. The chapters draw on research on men and women leaders in elementary, secondary and postsecondary schools in Australia, Canada, New Zealand, Sweden, the United Kingdom and the United States.

The authors counter essentialist claims about leaders that are based on biological, psychological and/or sociological theories that stress gender difference. Similarities between men and women and differences within gender groups are highlighted in this book. There are numerous discussions that employ sophisticated understandings of gender relations and leadership discourses in today's globalized context. Early scholarship on gender and leadership is supplemented here with more nuanced theories and explanations of how gender, race and class, for example, operate in connected and changing ways to affect the leadership experiences of men and women who work in different educational settings.

Contents:
*Introduction – **Part I: Leadership discourses and gender** – Negotiating and reconstructing gendered leadership discourses – Does size matter?: The interaction between principal gender, level of schooling and institutional scale in Australian schools – Gender and school leadership in Sweden – Gender and School leadership discourses: a Swedish perspective – **Part II: Leadership practices amidst global and local change** – Steel magnolias in velvet ghettoes: female leaders in Australian girl's schools – Influences of the discourses of globalization on mentoring for gender equity and social justice in educational leadership – Gender, leadership and change in faculties of education in three countries – **Part III: Disrupting the normative discourse of leadership** – Women performing the superintendency: problematizing the normative alignment of conceptions of power and constructions of gender – Considerations of leadership beyond the mind/body split – Transgressing heteronormativity in educational administration – Leadership and Aboriginal education in contemporary education: narratives of cognitive imperialism reconciling with decolonization – Bridge people: leaders for social justice – The Emperor has no clothes: professionalism, performativity and educational leadership in high risk postmodern times.*

Contributors:
Sandra Acker, Marie Battiste, Jill Blackmore, Cryss Brunner, John Collard, Marian Court, Anna Davis, Karin Franzen, Margaret Grogan, Olof Johannson, James Koschoreck, Betty Merchant, Cecilia Reynolds.

c.256pp 0 335 21440 1 (Paperback) 0 335 21441 X (Hardback)